Southern Living
Christmas
in the Kitchen

Southern Living

Christmas
in the Kitchen

The ultimate guide to cooking for the holidays

Oxmoor House

Hardcover ISBN-13: 978-0-8487-3735-1
Hardcover ISBN-10: 0-8487-3735-0
Softcover ISBN-13: 978-0-8487-3736-8
Softcover ISBN-10: 0-8487-3736-9
Printed in the United States of America
First Printing 2012

Oxmoor House

VP, Publishing Director: Jim Childs
Editorial Director: Leah McLaughlin
Creative Director: Felicity Keane
Senior Brand Manager: Daniel Fagan
Senior Editor: Rebecca Brennan
Managing Editor: Rebecca Benton

Southern Living Christmas in the Kitchen

Editor: Susan Ray
Project Editor: Emily Chappell
Assistant Designer: Allison Sperando Potter
Director, Test Kitchen: Elizabeth Tyler Austin
Assistant Directors, Test Kitchen: Julie Christopher,
  Julie Gunter
Recipe Developers and Testers: Wendy Ball, R.D.;
  Victoria E. Cox; Stefanie Maloney; Callie Nash;
  Leah Van Deren
Recipe Editor: Alyson Moreland Haynes
Food Stylists: Margaret Monroe Dickey,
  Catherine Crowell Steele
Photography Director: Jim Bathie
Senior Photo Stylist: Kay E. Clarke
Photo Stylist: Katherine Eckert Coyne
Assistant Photo Stylist: Mary Louise Menendez
Senior Production Manager: Greg A. Amason

Contributors

Compositor: Carol Loria
Copy Editors: Norma Butterworth-McKittrick,
  Barry Wise Smith
Proofreader: Rhonda Lee Lother
Indexer: Mary Ann Laurens
Recipe Developers and Testers: Erica Hopper,
  Kathleen Royal Phillips
Interns: Erin Bishop, Mackenzie Cogle, Laura Hoxworth,
  Ashley White

Southern Living

Editor: M. Lindsay Bierman
Executive Editors: Rachel Hardage Barrett,
  Jessica S. Thuston
Food Director: Shannon Sliter Satterwhite
Test Kitchen Director: Rebecca Kracke Gordon
Senior Writer: Donna Florio
Senior Food Editor: Mary Allen Perry
Recipe Editor: JoAnn Weatherly
Assistant Recipe Editor: Ashley Arthur
Test Kitchen Specialist/Food Styling:
  Vanessa McNeil Rocchio
Test Kitchen Professionals: Norman King, Pam Lolley,
  Angela Sellers
Homes Editor: Jennifer Kopf
Decorating Editor: Lindsey Ellis Beatty
Director, Editorial Licensing: Katie Terrell Morrow
Assistant Homes Editor: Zoë Gowen
Travel Editors: James T. Black, Kim Cross
Features Editor: Jennifer V. Cole
Senior Photographers: Ralph Anderson, Gary Clark,
  Art Meripol
Photographer: Robbie Caponetto, Laurey W. Glenn
Photo Research Coordinator: Ginny P. Allen
Senior Photo Stylist: Buffy Hargett
Editorial Assistants: Cory Bordonaro, Marian Cooper,
  Stephanie Granada, Pat York

Time Home Entertainment Inc.

Publisher: Richard Fraiman
VP, Strategy & Business Development:
  Steven Sandonato
Executive Director, Marketing Services: Carol Pittard
Executive Director, Retail & Special Sales:
  Tom Mifsud
Director, Bookazine Development & Marketing:
  Laura Adam
Publishing Director: Joy Butts
Finance Director: Glenn Buonocore
Associate General Counsel: Helen Wan

To order additional publications,
call **1-800-765-6400** or **1-800-491-0551.**

For more books to enrich your life,
visit **oxmoorhouse.com**

To search, savor, and share thousands of recipes,
visit **myrecipes.com**

Cover: Chocolate-Coffee Cheesecake (page 235)

Holiday Guide

*Holiday entertaining and gift-giving gets
even easier with these clever ideas.*

Contents

Entertaining

As the Christmas season approaches, we often become so caught up in the stress and hustle of preparing for the big day that we forget Christmas is a time to celebrate with friends and family. Entertaining can be easy (and fun) when you take the right steps to plan ahead. With party-ready recipes and smart ideas, you can host a memorable Christmas party. So get busy planning and you're on your way to throwing a memorable event everyone can look forward to this holiday season.

Planning Made Easy

A few days before your party, decide where you want to entertain guests and where you want them to gather. Set up those areas as serving spots by beginning to put out the platters, serving pieces, and decorations that you plan to use. If it is a sit-down dinner, set the table.

The following pages are filled with ideas and menus for your next event. When creating your own menu, keep in mind the varying tastes of your guests, and plan to serve a variety of food and drinks that everyone can enjoy. You don't have to offer 12 different appetizers to suit everyone. Just be sure to include several vegetarian, meat, and seafood offerings to provide options for all of your guests.

When deciding on drinks to serve at your soiree, remember to provide at least one nonalcoholic option. Mix up a fabulous, fruity cocktail for a fun, festive change from the usual wine or beer picks. These drinks can be made in advance by waiting to add alcohol just before serving. You can also double your recipe to make one mix minus the spirits.

Don't be afraid to ask for help. Another way to plan ahead so that your event runs smoothly is to get everyone involved in the process. Having each guest bring a dish or appetizer gives greater variety to your party or meal and takes pressure off the hostess to prepare everything. Just plan your menu in advance so that guests have plenty of time to prepare their part.

Continued on next page

While all of your guests may not be up for trying a new appetizer, a fruit or veggie tray paired with a cool, creamy dip makes for an excellent appetizer that can be prepared ahead and kept in the fridge until party time. Pour a can of cocktail nuts into a glass or silver bowl for a quick nibble that's ready in no time. Or prepare a tray of your favorite cheese with some specialty nuts and breadsticks.

Menu Preparation

Another important party tool is knowing when and how you will cook each dish. Because you can't fit five casseroles into one oven, it's essential to plan when each dish needs to go in. Sit down at least a week before your event and assemble a timetable to keep you on track for the big day. This will ensure that all of your dishes will be ready to serve on time and at the correct temperature.

It helps to plan on serving several dishes that can be made in advance. Most casseroles can be frozen weeks ahead of time, as can many breads and rolls. Just remember to transfer dishes to the refrigerator the night before so they have time to thaw before cooking.

Finally, after all the planning is done and the food and drinks are taken care of, don't forget to take a deep breath and allow yourself to enjoy the effort and preparation you've put forth. No party is fun when you are stressing over minor hiccups. Holiday get-togethers are all about what the name suggests, getting together and relaxing over food and drink. Great memories can be made regardless of how lavish an affair may be. Don't panic if your party or dinner doesn't go exactly as planned. Simply savor the time as a wonderful opportunity to enjoy the ones you're with.

Gifts from the Kitchen

It's true what they say: The best (and tastiest) gifts come from the heart. When deciding what to give to family and friends, look no further than your own cozy kitchen. Food gifts are perfect for that friend who has everything or a neighbor with whom you want to share a little something. When it comes to making gracious gifts to delight, the possibilities are endless, and some are even easier than you might imagine. Buttery breads and luscious cakes are the go-to gifts for busy cooks. Baked breads are always enjoyed right out the oven, but you can freeze them to use later as last-minute gifts for friends or neighbors or to share with guests.

Package with Panache

A little creativity can go a long way when it comes to presenting your food gifts. Decorative glass jars or pretty gift boxes from your local crafts store serve as perfect packaging for your presents and can be collected year-round. Simply wrap with cellophane for added shine, or top with a bow for a pretty presentation.

Reusing metal tins is a smart way to wrap up your holiday gift-giving. Tins of all shapes and sizes can be lined with colorful tissue paper and are the perfect size for sharing Christmas cookies or fudge.

Make-Ahead Magic

Make gifts a month or two before the holidays, and freeze them to make the season a little less stressful. Good food choices for freezing include breads, cookies, shredded cheese, crumb toppings, and soups and stews. Prevent freezer burn by choosing the proper container size for the amount of food you are freezing and tightly sealing to prevent excess air from entering the container. Do not refreeze cooked dishes that have already been frozen and reheated—this affects the flavor and the nutrients.

Treats for Early Risers

*Celebrate the magic of the morning with
a table full of taste-tempting breads, casseroles,
and other favorites.*

Brunch Punch

MAKES: about 3 qt. ✳ **HANDS-ON TIME:** 10 min. ✳ **TOTAL TIME:** 2 hr., 10 min.

1 (46-oz.) can pineapple juice
3 cups orange juice
2 cups cranberry juice

¾ cup powdered sugar
¼ cup lime juice

1. Stir together all ingredients. Cover and chill 2 hours. Stir before serving.

Hot Chocolate with Almond Liqueur

MAKES: 5 cups ✳ **HANDS-ON TIME:** 10 min. ✳ **TOTAL TIME:** 18 min.

¼ cup boiling water
⅓ cup chocolate syrup

4 cups milk
⅓ cup almond liqueur

1. Stir together boiling water and chocolate syrup in a medium saucepan; add milk, stirring until blended. Cook over medium heat 6 to 8 minutes or until thoroughly heated. Remove from heat, and stir in liqueur.

Note: We tested with Amaretto almond liqueur.

TRY THIS TWIST!

Hot Chocolate with Hazelnut Liqueur: Substitute hazelnut liqueur for almond liqueur. Proceed with recipe as directed.

Note: We tested with Frangelico hazelnut liqueur.

Skewered Fruit with Rum Drizzle

MAKES: 8 servings ❋ **HANDS-ON TIME:** 35 min. ❋ **TOTAL TIME:** 1 hr., 15 min.

8 to 10 (6-inch) wooden or metal skewers
2 bananas, cut into ½-inch slices
1 Tbsp. lemon juice
½ pineapple, peeled and cut into 1-inch pieces

2 star fruit, cut into ½-inch pieces
2 Tbsp. sugar
¼ tsp. ground cinnamon
2 Tbsp. dark rum
Garnishes: strawberries, pears, red currants

1. Soak wooden skewers in hot water 30 minutes. Toss banana slices with lemon juice.
2. Thread banana slices, pineapple, and star fruit alternately onto skewers. Place on a wire rack in an aluminum foil-lined broiler pan. Cover and chill up to 8 hours, if desired.
3. Preheat oven to broil. Combine sugar and cinnamon; sprinkle over fruit.
4. Broil 4 inches from heat 5 minutes on each side or until lightly browned. Drizzle with rum. Garnish, if desired.

Morning Glory Muffins

MAKES: 2 dozen ❊ **HANDS-ON TIME:** 30 min. ❊ **TOTAL TIME:** 1 hr., 33 min.

1	cup chopped pecans	¾	cup canola oil
3	cups all-purpose flour	3	large eggs
1	tsp. salt	2½	tsp. vanilla extract
1	tsp. baking soda	1	(8-oz.) can crushed pineapple, undrained
1	tsp. ground cinnamon		
½	tsp. ground nutmeg	2	large carrots, finely grated (1 cup)
2	cups sugar	1	cup golden raisins

1. Preheat oven to 350°. Bake pecans in a single layer on a baking sheet 5 to 7 minutes or until lightly toasted and fragrant. Cool completely on a wire rack (about 15 minutes).

2. Meanwhile, combine flour, salt, baking soda, ground cinnamon, and nutmeg in a large bowl; make a well in center of mixture.

3. Whisk together sugar, canola oil, eggs, and vanilla; fold in crushed pineapple and carrots. Add to flour mixture, stirring just until dry ingredients are moistened. Fold in toasted pecans and raisins. Spoon into 2 lightly greased (12-cup) muffin pans, filling two-thirds full.

4. Bake at 350° for 23 to 25 minutes or until a wooden pick inserted in center comes out clean. Cool in pans on wire rack 5 minutes. Remove from pans to wire rack, and cool completely (about 30 minutes).

Note: Muffins may be made ahead and frozen in a zip-top plastic freezer bag up to 1 month, if desired. Remove from bag, and let thaw at room temperature.

test kitchen tips: muffin magic

1. The less muffin batter is stirred, the better. Overstirring results in muffins that are tough with undesirable tunnels inside.

2. If all of the cups aren't used when filling the muffin pan with batter, pour water into the empty cups to keep the pan from buckling.

Applesauce Muffins with Cinnamon Streusel Topping

MAKES: 1 dozen ✳ **HANDS-ON TIME:** 15 min. ✳ **TOTAL TIME:** 48 min.

4	cups all-purpose baking mix	½	cup milk
½	cup sugar	¼	cup vegetable oil
2	tsp. ground cinnamon	2	large eggs
⅔	cup chunky applesauce		Cinnamon Streusel Topping

1. Preheat oven to 400°. Whisk together baking mix, sugar, and cinnamon in a large bowl; make a well in center of mixture.

2. Whisk together applesauce and next 3 ingredients in a small bowl; add to sugar mixture, stirring just until dry ingredients are moistened. Spoon batter into a lightly greased (12-cup) muffin pan, filling almost completely full. Sprinkle Cinnamon Streusel Topping over batter.

3. Bake at 400° for 18 to 20 minutes or until a wooden pick inserted in center comes out clean and tops are golden brown. Cool in pan on a wire rack 5 minutes. Remove from pan to a wire rack, and cool completely.

Note: We tested with Bisquick Original Pancake and Baking Mix.

Cinnamon Streusel Topping

MAKES: about 1 cup ❋ **HANDS-ON TIME:** 10 min. ❋ **TOTAL TIME:** 10 min.

⅓ cup granulated sugar
¼ cup firmly packed light brown sugar
3 Tbsp. all-purpose baking mix

¼ tsp. ground cinnamon
2 Tbsp. butter, melted

1. Whisk together first 4 ingredients until blended. Stir melted butter into sugar mixture until well blended and crumbly.

Buttermilk-Poppy Seed Muffins

MAKES: 1 dozen ❋ **HANDS-ON TIME:** 15 min. ❋ **TOTAL TIME:** 45 min., including glaze

2 cups all-purpose flour
1 cup sugar
1 Tbsp. orange zest
1½ tsp. baking powder
½ tsp. baking soda
½ tsp. salt

1 cup buttermilk
3 large eggs
2 Tbsp. poppy seeds
1 tsp. vanilla extract
½ cup butter, melted
Orange Glaze

1. Preheat oven to 375°. Combine first 6 ingredients in a large bowl; make a well in center of mixture.
2. Whisk together buttermilk and next 3 ingredients in a medium bowl. Add buttermilk mixture to flour mixture, stirring just until dry ingredients are moistened. Stir in melted butter. Spoon batter into a lightly greased (12-cup) muffin pan, filling three-fourths full.
3. Bake at 375° for 20 to 25 minutes or until a wooden pick inserted in center comes out clean. Cool in pan on a wire rack 5 minutes. Remove from pans to a wire rack, and drizzle with Orange Glaze.

Orange Glaze

MAKES: about ½ cup ❋ **HANDS-ON TIME:** 5 min. ❋ **TOTAL TIME:** 5 min.

1 cup powdered sugar
1 tsp. vanilla extract

2 Tbsp. orange juice

1. Stir together powdered sugar, vanilla, and 1 Tbsp. orange juice. Stir in remaining 1 Tbsp. orange juice, 1 tsp. at a time, for desired consistency.

Bacon-and-Cheddar Corn Muffins

MAKES: 1 dozen ❋ **HANDS-ON TIME:** 22 min. ❋ **TOTAL TIME:** 52 min.

6   bacon slices
2   cups self-rising white cornmeal mix
1   Tbsp. sugar
1½   cups buttermilk
1   large egg

4   Tbsp. butter, melted
1   cup (4 oz.) shredded sharp Cheddar cheese
Vegetable cooking spray

1. Preheat oven to 425°. Cook bacon in a large skillet over medium-high heat 12 to 14 minutes or until crisp; remove bacon, and drain on paper towels. Crumble bacon.

2. Heat a (12-cup) muffin pan in oven 5 minutes.

3. Combine cornmeal mix and sugar in a medium bowl; make a well in center of mixture.

4. Stir together buttermilk and egg; add to cornmeal mixture, stirring just until dry ingredients are moistened. Stir in melted butter, cheese, and bacon. Remove pan from oven, and coat with cooking spray. Spoon batter into hot (12-cup) muffin pan, filling almost completely full.

5. Bake at 425° for 15 to 20 minutes or until golden. Remove from pan to a wire rack, and let cool 10 minutes.

Note: We tested with White Lily White Cornmeal Mix.

TRY THESE TWISTS!

Scrambled Egg Muffin Sliders: Prepare recipe as directed. Whisk together 8 large eggs, 1 Tbsp. water, and ½ tsp. Creole seasoning in a medium bowl. Melt 1 Tbsp. butter in a large nonstick skillet. Add egg mixture, and cook, without stirring, 2 to 3 minutes or until eggs begin to set on bottom. Gently draw cooked edges away from sides of pan to form large pieces. Cook, stirring occasionally, 4 to 5 minutes or until eggs are thickened and moist. (Do not overstir.) Cut muffins in half, and spoon eggs over bottom halves. Cover with top halves of muffins.

Ham-and-Swiss Corn Muffins: Substitute Swiss cheese for Cheddar cheese and 1 cup diced cooked ham for bacon. Reduce butter in batter to 3 Tbsp. Brown ham in remaining 1 Tbsp. melted butter in a nonstick skillet over medium-high heat 5 to 6 minutes. Proceed as directed, whisking in 2 Tbsp. Dijon mustard with buttermilk and egg.

Southwestern Chile-Cheese Corn Muffins: Omit bacon. Substitute pepper Jack cheese for Cheddar cheese. Proceed as directed, stirring in 1 (4.5-oz.) can chopped green chiles, drained, with cheese and butter.

Scrambled Egg
Muffin Sliders

Vanilla Scones

MAKES: 8 servings ✳ **HANDS-ON TIME:** 15 min. ✳ **TOTAL TIME:** 30 min.

These scones make great holiday gifts. You can even package them with your favorite flavored butter.

2	cups all-purpose flour	1	large egg
⅓	cup sugar	1	Tbsp. vanilla extract
2	tsp. baking powder	1	egg white
⅛	tsp. salt	1	tsp. water
½	cup butter, cut up	2	Tbsp. sparkling sugar
⅔	cup whipping cream		

1. Preheat oven to 425°. Combine first 4 ingredients. Cut butter into flour mixture with a pastry blender or fork until crumbly.

2. Whisk together whipping cream, egg, and vanilla; add to flour mixture, stirring just until dry ingredients are moistened.

3. Turn dough out onto a lightly floured surface; pat into an 8½-inch circle. Cut into 8 wedges, and place 1 inch apart on a lightly greased baking sheet.

4. Whisk together egg white and water; brush over tops of scones. Sprinkle with sparkling sugar.

5. Bake at 425° for 15 minutes or until golden brown.

Note: We used sparkling sugar, which has larger crystals, to give the scones a festive look. Sparkling sugar is available in stores that carry cake-decorating supplies and in gourmet grocery stores. Granulated sugar can be substituted for sparkling sugar, if desired.

Cinnamon-Pecan Coffee Cake

MAKES: 10 to 12 servings * **HANDS-ON TIME:** 15 min. * **TOTAL TIME:** 9 hr., 20 min.

1 cup sugar
1 Tbsp. ground cinnamon
1 (25-oz.) package frozen bread roll dough

½ cup butter, melted
1 cup chopped pecans
Brown Sugar Glaze

1. Combine sugar and cinnamon.

2. Dip frozen rolls in melted butter; roll in sugar mixture. Arrange rolls in a well-greased 10-inch tube pan; sprinkle with pecans. Cover and chill 8 hours or overnight.

3. Preheat oven to 325°. Pour Brown Sugar Glaze over dough.

4. Bake at 325° for 55 minutes or until done. Let stand 10 minutes. Invert onto a serving plate, and drizzle with remaining glaze in pan.

Note: We tested with Rich's Enriched Homestyle Roll Dough.

Brown Sugar Glaze

MAKES: about ¾ cup * **HANDS-ON TIME:** 5 min. * **TOTAL TIME:** 5 min.

½ cup whipping cream
½ cup firmly packed brown sugar

1 tsp. ground cinnamon

1. Beat whipping cream at high speed with an electric mixer until soft peaks form; stir in brown sugar and cinnamon.

Serve this dessert-like bread at a holiday brunch, or package it to give to neighbors.

Apricot-Pecan Cinnamon Sweet Rolls

MAKES: 1 dozen * **HANDS-ON TIME:** 15 min. * **TOTAL TIME:** 1 hr., 58 min.

1   (26.4-oz.) package frozen biscuits
1   (6-oz.) package dried apricots
All-purpose flour
¼   cup butter, softened
¾   cup firmly packed brown sugar

1   tsp. ground cinnamon
½   cup chopped pecans, toasted
1   cup powdered sugar
3   Tbsp. milk
½   tsp. vanilla extract

1. Preheat oven to 375°. Arrange frozen biscuits, with sides touching, in 3 rows of 4 biscuits on a lightly floured surface. Let stand 30 to 45 minutes or until biscuits are thawed but still cool to the touch.

2. Pour boiling water to cover over dried apricots, and let stand 10 minutes; drain well. Chop apricots.

3. Sprinkle thawed biscuits lightly with flour. Press biscuit edges together, and pat to form a 10- x 12-inch rectangle of dough; spread evenly with softened butter. Stir together brown sugar and cinnamon; sprinkle evenly over butter. Sprinkle chopped apricots and pecans evenly over brown sugar mixture.

4. Roll up, starting at one long end; cut into 12 (about 1-inch-thick) slices. Place rolls into a lightly greased 10-inch cast-iron skillet, 10-inch round cake pan, or 9-inch square pan.

5. Bake at 375° for 35 to 40 minutes or until center rolls are golden brown and done; cool slightly.

6. Stir together powdered sugar, milk, and vanilla; drizzle evenly over rolls.

Note: To prepare individual rolls, prepare as directed; place one slice in each of 12 lightly greased 3-inch muffin cups. Bake at 375° for 20 to 25 minutes or until golden brown. Cool slightly, and remove from pan.

TRY THESE TWISTS!

Cinnamon-Raisin Rolls: Prepare rolls as directed, substituting 1 cup golden raisins for 1 (6-oz.) package dried apricots.

Peaches-and-Cream Cinnamon Rolls: Prepare rolls as directed, substituting ½ (8-oz.) package softened cream cheese for ¼ cup butter and 1 (6-oz.) package dried peaches for 1 (6-oz.) package dried apricots.

Chocolate-Cherry-Cream Cheese Cinnamon Rolls: Prepare rolls as directed, substituting ½ (8-oz.) package softened cream cheese for ¼ cup butter, 1 (6-oz.) package dried cherries for 1 (6-oz.) package dried apricots, and 1 cup semisweet chocolate morsels for ½ cup pecans.

test kitchen tip: how to prepare sweet rolls

1. Arrange frozen biscuits, with sides touching, in 3 rows of 4 biscuits on a lightly floured surface. Let stand 30 to 45 minutes or until biscuits are thawed but still cool to the touch.

2. Sprinkle thawed biscuits with flour. Press edges together, and pat to form a 10-x 12-inch rectangle of dough.

3. Spread rectangle with butter or cream cheese, and sprinkle with desired fillings.

4. Roll up, starting at the long end of the rectangle and pressing together any open spaces on the underside of the dough as you roll.

5. Cut into 12 slices. (The rectangle of dough will elongate as it's rolled, yielding 12 slices that are each a little more than 1 inch thick.)

6. Place rolls into a lightly greased 10-inch cast-iron skillet or baking pan. (Variations can also be baked in 3-inch muffin cups. See Apricot-Pecan Cinnamon Sweet Rolls for directions.)

Pepper Jelly Danish

MAKES: 8 servings * **HANDS-ON TIME:** 25 min. * **TOTAL TIME:** 55 min.

4   (8-oz.) cans refrigerated crescent rolls
1   (8-oz.) package cream cheese, softened
1   large egg, lightly beaten

⅓   cup red pepper jelly
1   tablespoon honey

1. Preheat oven to 375°. Unroll 1 can crescent roll dough on a lightly floured surface; divide into 2 pieces, separating at center perforation. Press each piece into a 7-inch square, pressing perforations to seal.
2. Bring corners of each dough square to center, partially overlapping each; gently press corners into centers using thumb, making a small indentation. Repeat procedure with remaining cans of crescent rolls. Transfer to lightly greased baking sheets.
3. Stir together cream cheese and egg; stir together pepper jelly and honey. Spoon 2 Tbsp. cream cheese mixture into center of each dough circle, and top with 2 tsp. pepper jelly mixture.
4. Bake, in batches, at 375° for 15 to 18 minutes or until golden brown.

Holiday Cream Cheese Coffee Cake

MAKES: 8 servings * **HANDS-ON TIME:** 5 min. * **TOTAL TIME:** 35 min.

1   (11.5-oz.) frozen pecan coffee cake, thawed

4   oz. cream cheese, softened
¼   cup firmly packed dark brown sugar

1. Preheat oven to 350°. Remove coffee cake from package; remove and discard plastic overwrap.
2. Slice coffee cake in half horizontally. Spread softened cream cheese on bottom half of coffee cake; sprinkle with brown sugar. Place top layer of coffee cake right side up on bottom layer.
3. Bake at 350° for 15 to 20 minutes. Let cool on a wire rack 10 minutes.

Pepper Jelly
Danish

Country Ham and Biscuits

Bake frozen tea biscuits (Mary B's is one of our favorite brands), and fill with thin slices of country ham that have been browned in a hot skillet 1 to 2 minutes on each side. Have guests dress biscuits with flavored butter and mustard blends.

Blackberry Mustard

MAKES: about ⅔ cup ✳ **HANDS-ON TIME:** 5 min. ✳ **TOTAL TIME:** 5 min.

½ cup blackberry preserves

2 Tbsp. Dijon mustard

1. Stir together preserves and mustard.

Lemon-Herb Butter

MAKES: about ½ cup ✳ **HANDS-ON TIME:** 5 min. ✳ **TOTAL TIME:** 5 min.

½ cup butter, softened

2 Tbsp. chopped fresh parsley

2 tsp. chopped fresh chives

2 tsp. lemon zest

1. Stir together all ingredients.

The so-Southern combination of ham and biscuits is always a hit! These will be the first thing to disappear at your next holiday brunch.

Breakfast Enchiladas

MAKES: 8 servings ❋ **HANDS-ON TIME:** 35 min. ❋ **TOTAL TIME:** 1 hr., 21 min.

Serve this tasty breakfast dish alongside ingredients such as pico de gallo, tomatillo salsa, and sliced jalapeño.

1	(1-lb.) package hot ground pork sausage		Cheese Sauce
2	Tbsp. butter or margarine	8	(8-inch) flour tortillas
4	green onions, thinly sliced	1	cup (4 oz.) shredded pepper Jack
2	Tbsp. chopped fresh cilantro		cheese
14	large eggs, beaten		Toppings: halved grape tomatoes, sliced
¾	tsp. salt		green onions, chopped fresh cilantro
½	tsp. pepper		

1. Preheat oven to 350°. Cook sausage in a large nonstick skillet over medium-high heat, stirring until sausage crumbles and is no longer pink. Remove from pan; drain well, pressing between paper towels.

2. Melt butter in a large nonstick skillet over medium heat. Add green onions and cilantro, and sauté 1 minute. Add eggs, salt, and pepper, and cook, without stirring, until eggs begin to set on bottom. Draw a spatula across bottom of pan to form large curds. Continue to cook until eggs are thickened but still moist; do not stir constantly. Remove from heat, and gently fold in 1½ cups Cheese Sauce and sausage.

3. Spoon about ⅓ cup egg mixture down the center of each flour tortilla; roll up. Place, seam side down, in a lightly greased 13- x 9-inch baking dish. Pour remaining Cheese Sauce evenly over tortillas; sprinkle evenly with pepper Jack cheese.

4. Bake at 350° for 30 minutes or until sauce is bubbly. Serve with desired toppings.

Cheese Sauce

MAKES: about 4 cups ❋ **HANDS-ON TIME:** 18 min. ❋ **TOTAL TIME:** 18 min.

⅓	cup butter	1	(4.5-oz.) can chopped green chiles,
⅓	cup flour		undrained
3	cups milk	¾	tsp. salt
2	cups (8 oz.) shredded Cheddar cheese		

1. Melt butter in a heavy saucepan over medium-low heat; whisk in flour until smooth. Cook, whisking constantly, 1 minute. Gradually whisk in milk; cook over medium heat, whisking constantly, 5 minutes or until thickened. Remove from heat, and whisk in remaining ingredients.

Hominy Grill's Shrimp and Grits

MAKES: 6 servings ❋ **HANDS-ON TIME:** 30 min. ❋ **TOTAL TIME:** 49 min.

2   lb. unpeeled, medium-size raw shrimp (31/40 count)
2   Tbsp. all-purpose flour
5   bacon slices, chopped
1   (8-oz.) package sliced fresh mushrooms
3   garlic cloves, minced

⅓   cup fresh lemon juice
½   cup thinly sliced green onions
2   tsp. hot sauce
½   tsp. salt
Creamy Cheddar Cheese Grits

1. Peel shrimp; devein, if desired. Toss shrimp with flour until lightly coated, shaking to remove excess.

2. Cook bacon in a medium skillet over medium-high heat 8 to 10 minutes or until crisp. Remove bacon, and drain on paper towels, reserving drippings in skillet.

3. Sauté mushrooms in hot drippings 4 minutes or just until mushrooms begin to release their liquid. Add shrimp, and sauté 3 to 3½ minutes or just until shrimp turn pink. Add garlic, and sauté 1 minute (do not brown garlic). Add lemon juice and next 3 ingredients; serve immediately over Creamy Cheddar Cheese Grits. Sprinkle with bacon.

Creamy Cheddar Cheese Grits

MAKES: 8½ cups ❋ **HANDS-ON TIME:** 10 min. ❋ **TOTAL TIME:** 1 hr., 45 min.

4   Tbsp. butter
5   cups milk
2   tsp. salt
½   tsp. hot sauce

1   garlic clove, pressed
1½   cups uncooked stone-ground white grits
1   (10-oz.) block sharp white Cheddar cheese, grated

1. Bring 2 Tbsp. butter, next 4 ingredients, and 5 cups water to a boil in a medium-size Dutch oven over medium-high heat. Gradually whisk in grits, and bring to a boil. Reduce heat to medium-low, and simmer, stirring occasionally, 1½ hours or until thickened. Stir in cheese and remaining 2 Tbsp. butter until melted. Serve immediately.

TRY THIS TWIST!

Quick-Cooking Creamy Cheddar Cheese Grits: Substitute 2 cups uncooked quick-cooking grits for stone-ground grits. Decrease water and milk to 4½ cups each. Prepare recipe as directed, cooking grits 10 to 15 minutes or until thickened.

Hominy Grill's
Shrimp and Grits

Brie-and-Veggie Breakfast Strata

MAKES: 8 to 10 servings ✻ **HANDS-ON TIME:** 40 min. ✻ **TOTAL TIME:** 9 hr., 25 min.

1 large sweet onion, halved and thinly sliced	1 cup (4 oz.) shredded Parmesan cheese
1 large red bell pepper, diced	8 large eggs
1 large Yukon gold potato, peeled and diced	3 cups milk
2 Tbsp. olive oil	2 Tbsp. Dijon mustard
1 (8-oz.) Brie round*	1 tsp. seasoned salt
1 (12-oz.) package sourdough bread loaf, cubed	1 tsp. pepper

1. Sauté first 3 ingredients in hot oil 10 to 12 minutes or just until vegetables are tender and onion slices begin to turn golden.

2. Trim and discard rind from Brie. Cut cheese into ½-inch cubes.

3. Layer a lightly greased 13- x 9-inch baking dish with half each of bread cubes, onion mixture, Brie cubes, and Parmesan cheese.

4. Whisk together eggs and next 4 ingredients; pour half of egg mixture evenly over cheeses. Repeat layers once. Cover and chill at least 8 hours or up to 24 hours.

5. Preheat oven to 350°. Bake 45 to 50 minutes or until lightly browned on top and set in center.

*2 cups (8 oz.) shredded Swiss cheese may be substituted.

Individual Country
Grits-and-Sausage Casseroles

MAKES: 10 servings ❖ **HANDS-ON TIME:** 30 min. ❖ **TOTAL TIME:** 1 hr., 32 min.

1 lb. mild ground pork sausage
1 lb. hot ground pork sausage
1¼ cups uncooked quick-cooking grits
3 cups (12 oz.) shredded Cheddar-Jack cheese

1 cup milk
½ tsp. garlic salt
4 large eggs, lightly beaten
Paprika

1. Preheat oven to 350°. Brown mild and hot sausages in a large skillet, stirring often, 6 to 8 minutes or until meat crumbles and is no longer pink; drain well, and pat with paper towels.

2. Bring 4 cups water to a boil in a large saucepan; gradually stir in grits. Return to a boil; cover, reduce heat, and simmer, stirring occasionally, 5 minutes. Remove from heat; add cheese, milk, and garlic salt, stirring until cheese melts. Stir in sausage and eggs. Spoon mixture into 10 (8-oz.) lightly greased ramekins; sprinkle with paprika.

3. Bake at 350° for 45 to 50 minutes or until golden and mixture is set. Let stand 10 minutes before serving.

To Make Ahead: Prepare recipe as directed through Step 2. Cover ramekins tightly, and chill overnight. Uncover and let stand 30 minutes. Bake as directed.

TRY THIS TWIST!

Lightened Country Grits-and-Sausage Casseroles: Substitute 2 (12-oz.) packages 50% reduced-fat ground pork sausage for 2 lb. sausage, 3 cups shredded 2% reduced-fat sharp Cheddar cheese for Cheddar-Jack cheese, 1% low-fat milk for whole milk, and 1 cup egg substitute for eggs.

Celebrate Christmas morning with this tasty, make-ahead casserole that makes enough for a crowd.

Tomato-Herb Frittata

MAKES: 6 to 8 servings ✷ **HANDS-ON TIME:** 27 min. ✷ **TOTAL TIME:** 44 min.

2   Tbsp. olive oil
1   garlic clove, minced
½   (6-oz.) package fresh baby spinach
1   (10-oz.) can mild diced tomatoes and
    green chiles, drained

¼   tsp. salt
¼   tsp. pepper
12 large eggs, beaten*
½   cup crumbled garlic-and-herb
    feta cheese**

1. Preheat oven to 350°. Heat oil in a 10-inch (2-inch-deep) ovenproof nonstick skillet over medium-high heat.
2. Add garlic, and sauté 1 minute. Stir in spinach, and cook, stirring constantly, 1 minute or just until spinach begins to wilt.
3. Add tomatoes and green chiles, salt, and pepper; cook, stirring frequently, 2 to 3 minutes or until spinach is wilted. Add eggs, and sprinkle with cheese. Cook 3 to 5 minutes, gently lifting edges of frittata with a spatula and tilting pan so uncooked portion flows underneath.
4. Bake at 350° for 12 to 15 minutes or until set and lightly browned. Remove from oven, and let stand 5 minutes. Slide frittata onto a large platter, and cut into 8 wedges.

*1 (32-oz.) carton egg substitute may be substituted. Increase bake time to 16 to 18 minutes or until set.
**Plain feta cheese may be substituted.

Note: We tested with Ro-Tel Mild Diced Tomatoes & Green Chiles.

TRY THESE TWISTS!

Tomato-Sausage Frittata: Brown ½ lb. ground pork sausage in a 10-inch (2-inch-deep) ovenproof nonstick skillet over medium-high heat, stirring often, 7 to 8 minutes or until meat crumbles and is no longer pink; remove from skillet, and drain. Wipe skillet clean. Proceed with recipe as directed, adding sausage with tomatoes and green chiles in Step 3.

Bacon-Mushroom Frittata: Prepare recipe as directed in Step 1, sautéing ½ cup sliced fresh mushrooms in hot oil 2 to 3 minutes or until browned. Proceed with recipe as directed, stirring 3 cooked and chopped bacon slices in with tomatoes.

Eggplant-and-Olive Frittata: Prepare recipe as directed in Step 1, sautéing 1 cup peeled and chopped eggplant 5 minutes or until tender. Proceed with recipe as directed, stirring ½ cup sliced black olives in with tomatoes.

Tomato-Herb Frittata

Merry Starters

Welcome guests with tasty appetizers and beverages perfect for any type of celebration.

Banana-Pecan
Smoothie

Banana-Pecan Smoothie

MAKES: 4 cups ❋ **HANDS-ON TIME:** 10 min. ❋ **TOTAL TIME:** 10 min.

1½	cups low-fat vanilla yogurt	½	cup milk
2	large ripe bananas, sliced and frozen	1	Tbsp. honey
1	cup ice	½	tsp. ground cinnamon
½	cup finely chopped toasted pecans		

1. Process all ingredients in a blender until smooth. Pour into glasses, and serve immediately.

Brandy Slush

MAKES: 19 cups ❋ **HANDS-ON TIME:** 15 min. ❋ **TOTAL TIME:** 4 hr., 35 min.

9	cups boiling water, divided	1	(12-oz.) can frozen lemonade concentrate, thawed
4	regular-size tea bags		
2	cups sugar	1⅔	cups brandy
1	(12-oz.) can frozen orange juice concentrate, thawed	¼	cup lime juice
		4	(10-oz.) bottles club soda, chilled

1. Pour 2 cups boiling water over tea bags; cover and let steep 5 minutes. Remove and discard tea bags, squeezing gently.

2. Stir together remaining 7 cups boiling water and 2 cups sugar in a Dutch oven, stirring until sugar dissolves. Stir in tea mixture, orange juice concentrate, and next 3 ingredients. Let cool to room temperature (about 30 minutes). Divide mixture between 2 (1-gal.) zip-top plastic freezer bags; freeze 4 hours.

3. Remove bags from freezer 30 minutes before serving. Squeeze 1 bag with hands to break mixture into chunks; pour into a pitcher, and stir in 2 bottles club soda until slushy. Repeat with remaining bag.

Frozen Sangría

MAKES: about 1½ gal. ✱ **HANDS-ON TIME:** 10 min. ✱ **TOTAL TIME:** 24 hr., 10 min.

1   gal. sangría

1   (12-oz.) can frozen limeade, thawed

1   (2-liter) bottle lemon-lime soft drink

2   cups sliced oranges, lemons, and limes

1. Place 1 (2-gal.) zip-top plastic freezer bag inside another 2-gal. zip-top plastic freezer bag. Place bags in a large bowl. Combine sangría, limeade, and lemon-lime soft drink in the inside bag. Seal both bags, and freeze 24 hours. (Double bagging is a precaution to avoid spills.)

2. Remove mixture from freezer 1 hour before serving, squeezing occasionally until slushy. Transfer mixture to a 2-gal. container. Stir in fruit.

TRY THIS TWIST!

Kid-Friendly Frozen Sangría: Substitute cranberry juice for sangría. Proceed with recipe as directed.

Mock Tea Sangría

MAKES: 9 cups ✱ **HANDS-ON TIME:** 25 min. ✱ **TOTAL TIME:** 2 hr., 30 min.

1   (10-oz.) package frozen raspberries, thawed

⅓   cup sugar

1   family-size tea bag

2   cups red grape juice

1   lemon, sliced

1   lime, sliced

1   (16-oz.) bottle orange soft drink, chilled

1. Process raspberries in a blender or food processor until smooth, stopping to scrape down sides. Pour puree through a fine wire-mesh strainer into a large container, discarding raspberry seeds.

2. Bring sugar and 3 cups water to a boil in a saucepan, stirring often. Remove from heat; add tea bag. Cover and steep 5 minutes.

3. Remove tea bag with a slotted spoon, squeezing gently; cool tea mixture slightly. Stir together raspberry puree, tea mixture, grape juice, and lemon and lime slices. Cover and chill 2 to 24 hours. Stir in orange soft drink, and serve immediately over ice.

Mock Tea
Sangría

Frozen
Sangría

Carolina Peach Sangría

Carolina Peach Sangría

MAKES: about 9 cups ❊ **HANDS-ON TIME:** 10 min. ❊ **TOTAL TIME:** 8 hr., 10 min.

1	(750-milliliter) bottle rosé wine	2	Tbsp. sugar
¾	cup vodka*	2	(16-oz.) packages frozen sliced peaches, peeled
½	cup peach nectar		
6	Tbsp. thawed frozen lemonade concentrate	1	(6-oz.) package fresh raspberries**
		2	cups club soda, chilled

1. Combine first 5 ingredients in a pitcher; stir until sugar is dissolved. Stir in peaches and raspberries. Cover and chill 8 hours.

2. Stir in chilled club soda just before serving.

*Peach-flavored vodka may be substituted. Omit peach nectar.

**1 cup frozen raspberries may be substituted.

Classic Margarita on the Rocks

MAKES: 1½ cups ❊ **HANDS-ON TIME:** 10 min. ❊ **TOTAL TIME:** 10 min.

Lime wedge		½	cup powdered sugar
Margarita salt		½	cup fresh lime juice (about 3 limes)
¾	cup tequila	¼	cup orange liqueur

1. Rub rims of 4 chilled margarita glasses with lime wedge; dip rims in salt to coat. Fill glasses with ice.

2. Stir together tequila and next 3 ingredients in a small pitcher, stirring until sugar dissolves.

3. Fill a cocktail shaker half full with ice. Add desired amount of margarita mixture, cover with lid, and shake until thoroughly chilled. Strain into prepared glasses. Serve immediately.

Note: We tested with Jose Cuervo Especial for tequila and Triple Sec for orange liqueur.

TRY THESE TWISTS!

Pomegranate Margaritas: Decrease lime juice to ¼ cup. Stir ½ cup pomegranate juice into tequila mixture in Step 2. Makes about 2 cups.

Strawberry Margaritas: Substitute red decorator sugar crystals for margarita salt. Reduce powdered sugar to ¼ to ⅓ cup and lime juice to ¼ cup. Process 1 (10-oz.) package frozen strawberries in light syrup, thawed, in blender 30 seconds or until strawberries are smooth. Stir strawberry puree into tequila mixture in Step 2.

Spiced Pomegranate Sipper

MAKES: about 8 cups ✳ **HANDS-ON TIME:** 27 min. ✳ **TOTAL TIME:** 32 min.

1 (2½-inch-long) cinnamon stick
5 whole cloves
5 thin fresh ginger slices
2 (16-oz.) bottles refrigerated 100% pomegranate juice

4 cups white grape juice
½ cup pineapple juice
Garnishes: pineapple chunks, orange rind curls

1. Cook first 3 ingredients in a Dutch oven over medium heat, stirring constantly, 2 to 3 minutes or until cinnamon is fragrant.

2. Gradually stir in juices. Bring to a boil over medium-high heat; reduce heat to medium-low, and simmer 15 minutes. Pour mixture through a wire-mesh strainer into a heatproof pitcher; discard solids. Serve warm. Garnish, if desired.

Note: We tested with POM Wonderful 100% Pomegranate Juice and Welch's 100% White Grape Juice.

TRY THESE TWISTS!

Tipsy Hot Spiced Pomegranate Sipper: Prepare recipe as directed. Stir in 1¼ cups almond liqueur just before serving.

Cold Spiced Pomegranate Sipper: Prepare recipe as directed. Let stand 30 minutes. Cover and chill 2 hours. Store in refrigerator up to 2 days. Stir and serve over ice.

Fizzy Spiced Pomegranate Sipper: Prepare Cold Spiced Pomegranate Sipper as directed. Stir in 1 (33.8-oz.) bottle ginger ale just before serving.

Spiced Pomegranate Sipper

Rudolph's Spritzer

MAKES: about 2 qt. ✳ **HANDS-ON TIME:** 10 min. ✳ **TOTAL TIME:** 10 min.

5   cups orange juice
2   cups chilled lemon-lime soft drink
½   cup maraschino cherry juice

¼   cup fresh lemon juice
Garnishes: lemon slices, fresh rosemary sprigs

1. Stir together first 4 ingredients; serve over ice. Garnish, if desired.

Rudolph's Tipsy Spritzer: Prepare recipe as directed. Stir in 1½ cups vodka. Makes about 9½ cups.

Raspberry-Beer Cocktail

MAKES: 6 servings ✳ **HANDS-ON TIME:** 5 min. ✳ **TOTAL TIME:** 5 min.

¾   cup frozen raspberries*
3½ (12-oz.) bottles beer, chilled
1   (12-oz.) container frozen raspberry
    lemonade concentrate, thawed

½   cup vodka

1. Stir together all ingredients. Serve over ice.

*Fresh raspberries may be substituted.

Note: To make ahead, stir together lemonade concentrate and vodka in a large container. Chill up to 3 days. Stir in raspberries and beer just before serving.

Rudolph's Spritzer

Rich 'n' Thick
Hot Chocolate

Rich 'n' Thick Hot Chocolate

MAKES: about 4 cups ❊ **HANDS-ON TIME:** 18 min.
TOTAL TIME: 28 min., including whipped cream

2 tsp. cornstarch
4 cups milk, divided
2 (3.5-oz.) dark chocolate bars
(at least 70% cacao), chopped

⅓ cup honey
1 tsp. vanilla extract
Pinch of salt
Marshmallow Whipped Cream (optional)

1. Whisk together cornstarch and ½ cup milk until smooth.

2. Cook remaining 3½ cups milk in a large, nonaluminum saucepan over medium heat until bubbles appear around edge of pan (about 4 minutes; do not boil). Whisk in chocolate, honey, vanilla extract, and salt until blended and smooth. Whisk in cornstarch mixture.

3. Bring milk mixture to a light boil, whisking frequently (about 4 minutes). Remove from heat. Cool slightly. (Mixture will thicken as it cools.) Serve immediately with Marshmallow Whipped Cream, if desired.

Note: We tested with Ghirardelli Intense Dark Twilight Delight 72% Cacao dark chocolate bar.

TRY THESE TWISTS!

Mexican Rich 'n' Thick Hot Chocolate: Prepare recipe as directed through Step 2, whisking in 1¼ tsp. ground cinnamon and 1 tsp. ancho chili powder with chocolate. Proceed with recipe as directed.

Orange-Almond Rich 'n' Thick Hot Chocolate: Prepare recipe as directed through Step 2, whisking in 3 Tbsp. orange juice and 2 Tbsp. almond liqueur with chocolate. Proceed with recipe as directed.

Note: We tested with Amaretto for almond liqueur.

Grown-up Rich 'n' Thick Hot Chocolate: Prepare recipe as directed through Step 2, whisking in ½ cup Southern Comfort with chocolate. Proceed with recipe as directed.

Marshmallow Whipped Cream

MAKES: about 1½ cups ❊ **HANDS-ON TIME:** 10 min. ❊ **TOTAL TIME:** 10 min.

½ cup whipping cream
1 Tbsp. powdered sugar

½ cup miniature marshmallows

1. Beat whipping cream at medium-high speed with an electric mixer until foamy; gradually add powdered sugar, beating until soft peaks form. Fold in marshmallows. Serve immediately, or cover and chill up to 2 hours.

Blue Cheese-Bacon Dip

Blue Cheese-Bacon Dip

MAKES: 12 to 15 servings ❋ **HANDS-ON TIME:** 36 min. ❋ **TOTAL TIME:** 56 min.

3 Tbsp. chopped walnuts

7 bacon slices, chopped

2 garlic cloves, minced

2 (8-oz.) packages cream cheese, softened

⅓ cup half-and-half

4 oz. crumbled blue cheese

2 Tbsp. chopped fresh chives

Grape clusters, pears, assorted crackers

1. Preheat oven to 350°. Bake walnuts in single layer in a shallow pan 6 to 8 minutes or until toasted and fragrant, stirring after 3 minutes.

2. Cook bacon in a large skillet over medium-high heat, stirring often, 10 minutes or until crisp. Remove bacon, and drain on paper towels, reserving 1 Tbsp. drippings in skillet. Add minced garlic to hot drippings, and sauté 1 minute.

3. Beat cream cheese at medium speed with an electric mixer until smooth. Add half-and-half, beating until combined. Stir in bacon, garlic, blue cheese, and chives. Spoon mixture into 4 (1-cup) baking dishes or 1 (1-qt.) baking dish.

4. Bake at 350° for 20 minutes or until golden and bubbly. Sprinkle with walnuts; serve with grapes, pears, and assorted crackers.

TRY THESE TWISTS!

Goat Cheese-Bacon Dip: Substitute pecans for walnuts, goat cheese for blue cheese, and 2 tsp. chopped fresh thyme for 2 Tbsp. chives. Serve with pear slices, toasted baguette slices, and assorted crackers.

Cheddar Cheese-Bacon Dip: Substitute pecans for walnuts, shredded sharp Cheddar cheese for blue cheese, and chopped fresh parsley for chives. Add ⅛ to ¼ tsp. ground red pepper, if desired.

This creamy dip goes a long way. Our staff uses it to top baked potatoes and grilled steak too.

Fresh Herb Sauce

MAKES: about 1½ cups ❋ **HANDS-ON TIME:** 10 min. ❋ **TOTAL TIME:** 10 min.

2 garlic cloves
1 (1-oz.) package fresh basil leaves, stems removed
4 mint sprigs, stems removed
1 cup firmly packed fresh flat-leaf parsley leaves (about 1 bunch)
½ cup grated Parmesan cheese

½ tsp. salt
½ tsp. freshly ground pepper
¼ cup warm water
½ cup olive oil
2 Tbsp. red wine vinegar
Assorted vegetables

1. Process garlic in a food processor 20 seconds or until minced. Add basil and next 5 ingredients; process 10 seconds.
2. Whisk together ¼ cup warm water, oil, and vinegar. With processor running, pour oil mixture through food chute in a slow, steady stream, processing just until blended. Serve with assorted vegetables.

Herbed Dip with Baby Vegetables

MAKES: 8 to 10 servings ❋ **HANDS-ON TIME:** 15 min. ❋ **TOTAL TIME:** 4 hr., 15 min.

1 cup mayonnaise
½ cup sour cream
2 Tbsp. chopped fresh parsley
1 Tbsp. finely chopped sweet onion
1 Tbsp. chopped fresh dill
1 tsp. Beau Monde seasoning

1 tsp. hot sauce
½ tsp. salt
1 lb. thin fresh asparagus
½ lb. haricots verts (tiny green beans), trimmed

1. Stir together first 8 ingredients in a small bowl until well blended. Cover and chill 4 to 24 hours.
2. Meanwhile, snap off and discard tough ends of asparagus. Cut asparagus into 6-inch pieces, reserving any remaining end portions for another use. Cook asparagus in boiling water to cover in a large saucepan 1 to 2 minutes or until crisp-tender; drain. Plunge into ice water to stop the cooking process; drain. Repeat procedure with haricots verts. Place vegetables in zip-top plastic bags; seal and chill until ready to serve. Serve mayonnaise mixture with chilled vegetables.

Fresh
Herb Sauce

Fresh Lemon-Basil Dip
with Blanched Green Beans

Fresh Lemon-Basil Dip with Blanched Green Beans

MAKES: about 25 servings ❋ **HANDS-ON TIME:** 30 min. ❋ **TOTAL TIME:** 30 min.

2   cups mayonnaise
1   cup chopped fresh basil
1   (8-oz.) container sour cream
2   Tbsp. lemon zest

¼   tsp. salt
6   lb. fresh green beans, trimmed
Garnishes: lemon zest, lemon slices

1. Whisk together first 5 ingredients until blended. Cover and chill until ready to serve. Cook beans, in batches, in boiling water to cover 3 to 5 minutes or until crisp-tender. Plunge into ice water to stop the cooking process; drain. Cover and chill beans until ready to serve. Serve dip with green beans. Garnish, if desired.

Smoky Ranch Dip

MAKES: about 1½ cups ❋ **HANDS-ON TIME:** 5 min. ❋ **TOTAL TIME:** 35 min.

1   (1-oz.) envelope Ranch dressing mix
1½   cups light sour cream
2   tsp. finely chopped canned chipotle peppers in adobo sauce

1   tsp. adobo sauce from can
Potato chips, assorted vegetables

1. Whisk together first 4 ingredients. Cover and chill 30 minutes. Serve with chips or assorted vegetables.

TRY THESE TWISTS!

Barbecue Ranch Dip: Omit chipotle peppers and adobo sauce. Stir in 2 Tbsp. barbecue sauce. Serve with roasted red new potatoes.

Lime-Cilantro Ranch Dip: Omit chipotle peppers and adobo sauce. Stir in 1 Tbsp. chopped fresh cilantro and 1 Tbsp. fresh lime juice. Serve with quesadillas, tacos, or chili.

Bacon-Onion Dip

MAKES 1¾ cups ✳ **HANDS-ON TIME:** 10 min. ✳ **TOTAL TIME:** 10 min.

1 (8-oz.) container sour cream	1 Tbsp. horseradish
½ cup cooked and crumbled bacon	2 tsp. fresh lemon juice
2 Tbsp. green onions, sliced	¼ tsp. pepper
3 Tbsp. buttermilk	½ tsp. salt

1. Stir together all ingredients. Cover and chill until ready to serve (up to 24 hours).

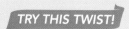

Blue Cheese-Bacon-Onion Dip: Stir in 1 (4-oz.) package crumbled blue cheese.

Bacon-Cheese Dip

MAKES: 1½ cups ✳ **HANDS-ON TIME:** 20 min. ✳ **TOTAL TIME:** 2 hr., 35 min.

½ cup sour cream	⅛ tsp. hot sauce
1 (4-oz.) package crumbled blue cheese	4 cooked bacon slices, crumbled
1 (3-oz.) package cream cheese, softened	Assorted crackers
2 Tbsp. diced onion	

1. Process first 5 ingredients in a blender or food processor until smooth, stopping to scrape down sides. Stir in half of bacon. Cover and chill 2 hours. Let stand at room temperature 15 minutes before serving. Sprinkle with remaining bacon. Serve with crackers.

Bacon-Cheese Dip

Blue Cheese "Hot Wing" Dip

Blue Cheese "Hot Wing" Dip

MAKES: about 3 cups ❋ **HANDS-ON TIME:** 10 min. ❋ **TOTAL TIME:** 1 hr., 10 min.

Try this spicy dip on burgers or tomatoes. We do not recommend fat-free products in this recipe.

1 (8-oz.) package ⅓-less-fat cream cheese, softened and cut into pieces
½ cup loosely packed fresh flat-leaf parsley leaves
¼ cup chopped green onions
¼ cup reduced-fat mayonnaise
¼ cup reduced-fat sour cream
2 Tbsp. white wine vinegar
1 garlic clove, minced

1 tsp. hot sauce
1 tsp. lemon zest
½ tsp. coarsely ground pepper
1 (4-oz.) package crumbled blue cheese
1 to 2 Tbsp. milk (optional)
Garnishes: crumbled blue cheese, chopped green onions, coarsely ground pepper
Chicken tenders, celery sticks, radishes, hot wing sauce

1. Pulse first 10 ingredients in a food processor 4 times or just until blended. Transfer mixture to a serving bowl, and gently stir in blue cheese. If desired, stir in 1 to 2 Tbsp. milk, 1 tsp. at a time, for desired consistency. Cover and chill 1 to 2 hours before serving. Garnish, if desired. Serve with chicken tenders, celery sticks, radishes, and hot wing sauce. Store leftovers in refrigerator up to 7 days.

Shrimp-and-Blue Cheese Spread

MAKES: 5½ cups ❋ **HANDS-ON TIME:** 30 min. ❋ **TOTAL TIME:** 4 hr., 45 min.

½ lb. unpeeled, large raw shrimp (21/25 count)*
¼ cup diced sweet onion
2 Tbsp. olive oil
½ (8-oz.) package cream cheese, softened
4 green onions, finely chopped
1 celery rib, finely chopped
1 cup crumbled blue cheese
1 cup mayonnaise

½ cup sour cream
2 Tbsp. chopped fresh parsley
2 tsp. lemon juice
1 tsp. Dijon mustard
½ tsp. salt
½ tsp. pepper
Assorted fresh vegetables
French bread baguette slices

1. Peel shrimp; devein, if desired.
2. Sauté onion in hot oil in a skillet over medium-high heat 3 minutes or until onion is tender. Stir in shrimp, and cook, stirring occasionally, 3 to 4 minutes or just until shrimp turn pink. Transfer to a bowl, and let stand 15 minutes. Chop shrimp, and return to bowl.
3. Stir in cream cheese and next 10 ingredients. Cover and chill 4 hours. Store in an airtight container up to 2 days. Serve with vegetables and bread slices.

*2½ lb. frozen unpeeled, large raw shrimp (21/25 count), thawed according to package directions, may be substituted.

Sweet 'n' Salty Honey-Cheese Spread

MAKES: 10 servings ✳ **HANDS-ON TIME:** 10 min. ✳ **TOTAL TIME:** 10 min.

1	(10.5-oz.) goat cheese log
½	cup roasted, salted sunflower seeds
⅓	cup honey
1	pt. fresh raspberries, blackberries, or blueberries

Garnish: fresh mint leaves
Assorted crackers

1. Press or roll goat cheese log in sunflower seeds, thoroughly covering cheese, including ends. Arrange cheese on a serving platter with any remaining sunflower seeds. Drizzle with honey. Sprinkle with berries. Garnish, if desired. Serve immediately with assorted crackers.

Blue Moon Inn Cheese Spread

MAKES: 8 servings ✳ **HANDS-ON TIME:** 15 min. ✳ **TOTAL TIME:** 20 min.

Store this spread in airtight container in refrigerator up to 4 days ahead.

½	cup pecans
¾	cup mayonnaise
½	cup pimiento-stuffed Spanish olives, chopped
⅓	cup bottled chili sauce

1	tsp. Worcestershire sauce
1	(10-oz.) block sharp Cheddar cheese, finely shredded

Vegetables, crackers

1. Preheat oven to 350°. Bake pecans in a single layer in a shallow pan 8 to 10 minutes or until toasted and fragrant. Cool 5 minutes; finely chop pecans.
2. Stir together mayonnaise and next 3 ingredients until well blended. Stir in cheese and pecans. Serve with vegetables and crackers.

Sweet 'n' Salty Honey-Cheese Spread

Warm Brie with Ginger-Citrus Glaze

MAKES: 6 to 8 servings ❋ **HANDS-ON TIME:** 10 min. ❋ **TOTAL TIME:** 17 min.

This appetizer will come together quickly. Pop the cheese in the oven, make your glaze in the microwave, and gather fresh fruit.

1	(8-oz.) Brie round	½	tsp. chopped fresh rosemary
¼	cup ginger preserves*	¼	tsp. salt
1	Tbsp. honey	¼	tsp. freshly ground pepper
2	tsp. apple cider vinegar		Assorted crackers, fresh fruit
1½	tsp. orange zest		

1. Preheat oven to 400°. Trim and discard rind from top of Brie. Place Brie on a lightly greased baking sheet. Bake 7 to 9 minutes or until cheese is just melted.

2. Meanwhile, microwave ginger preserves and next 6 ingredients in a small microwave-safe glass bowl at HIGH 30 seconds; stir until blended and smooth. Microwave at HIGH 1 minute. Let stand while cheese bakes.

3. Transfer Brie to a serving dish; immediately drizzle warm glaze over Brie. Serve with assorted crackers and fresh fruit.

*¼ cup fig preserves may be substituted.

Note: We tested with Dundee Ginger Preserve.

Place the Brie directly on an oven-safe serving plate, and bake as directed. The hot plate will keep the cheese warm and gooey longer.

Cornbread Tartlets with Tomato-Lima Bean Relish

MAKES: 2 dozen ✳ **HANDS-ON TIME:** 35 min. ✳ **TOTAL TIME:** 2 hr., 20 min., including relish

Inspired by summery succotash, these petite tarts are buttery and fresh all in one bite.

½   cup butter, softened
4   oz. cream cheese, softened
1¼   cups all-purpose flour
½   cup plain white cornmeal

¼   tsp. salt
Tomato-Lima Bean Relish
Garnish: crumbled goat cheese

1. Beat butter and cream cheese at medium speed with a heavy-duty electric stand mixer until creamy. Combine flour and next 2 ingredients in a small bowl. Gradually add flour mixture to butter mixture, beating at low speed just until blended. Shape dough into 24 balls, and place dough balls on a baking sheet; cover and chill 1 hour.

2. Preheat oven to 400°. Place 1 dough ball into each of 24 greased assorted-shape tartlet cups; press dough into cups and all the way up sides, forming shells.

3. Bake at 400° for 15 to 17 minutes or until edges are golden. Carefully remove pastry shells from cups to wire racks, and cool completely (about 15 minutes). Let stand at room temperature up to 4 hours before filling, if desired.

4. Spoon 1 rounded tablespoonful Tomato-Lima Bean Relish into each pastry shell. Garnish, if desired.

Tomato-Lima Bean Relish

MAKES: about 2 cups ✳ **HANDS-ON TIME:** 15 min. ✳ **TOTAL TIME:** 15 min.

1   cup cooked baby lima beans
¾   cup sliced grape tomatoes
3   Tbsp. finely chopped red onion

2   Tbsp. olive oil
2   tsp. red wine vinegar
Salt and pepper to taste

1. Stir together lima beans and next 4 ingredients. Season with salt and pepper to taste.

Coconut Shrimp

MAKES: 4 servings ❋ **HANDS-ON TIME:** 20 min. ❋ **TOTAL TIME:** 30 min.

Serve with your favorite honey mustard sauce for dipping.

1½ lb. unpeeled, large raw shrimp (21/25 count)
Vegetable cooking spray
2 egg whites
¼ cup cornstarch

1 Tbsp. Caribbean jerk seasoning
1 cup sweetened flaked coconut
1 cup panko (Japanese breadcrumbs)
1 tsp. paprika

1. Preheat oven to 425°. Peel shrimp, leaving tails on; devein shrimp, if desired.

2. Place a wire rack coated with cooking spray in a 15- x 10-inch jelly-roll pan.

3. Whisk egg whites in a bowl just until foamy.

4. Stir together cornstarch and Caribbean jerk seasoning in a shallow dish.

5. Stir together coconut, panko, and paprika in another shallow dish.

6. Dredge shrimp, 1 at a time, in cornstarch mixture; dip in egg whites, and dredge in coconut mixture, pressing gently with fingers. Lightly coat shrimp with cooking spray; arrange shrimp on wire rack.

7. Bake at 425° for 10 to 12 minutes or just until shrimp turn pink, turning after 8 minutes.

test kitchen tip: how to separate egg whites

■ Start with chilled eggs, as they are easier to separate without breaking the yolks. Gently crack the egg, keeping the shell together. Hold a cupped hand over a bowl. With the other, gently separate the shell along the crack, letting the yolk and white drip into your waiting hand. Keeping the solid yolk in your hand, allow the white to fall through your fingers into the bowl below.

Savory Hand Pies

MAKES: 18 pies ✳ **HANDS-ON TIME:** 30 min. ✳ **TOTAL TIME:** 48 min.

1 cup finely chopped roasted turkey
¾ cup mashed potatoes
½ (8-oz.) package cream cheese, softened
½ cup cut green beans, cooked
1 carrot, grated
2 Tbsp. chopped fresh parsley

Salt and pepper
1½ (14.1-oz.) packages refrigerated piecrusts
1 large egg, beaten
Poppy seeds (optional)
Turkey gravy, warmed

1. Stir together first 6 ingredients. Season with desired amount of salt and pepper.

2. Preheat oven to 400°. Unroll each piecrust. Lightly roll each into a 12-inch circle. Cut each piecrust into 6 circles using a 4-inch round cutter. Place about 3 Tbsp. turkey mixture just below center of each dough circle. Fold dough over filling, pressing and folding edges to seal.

3. Arrange pies on a lightly greased baking sheet. Brush with egg, and, if desired, sprinkle with poppy seeds.

4. Bake at 400° for 18 to 20 minutes or until golden brown. Serve with warm gravy.

Note: Unbaked pies can be frozen up to 1 month. Bake frozen pies 30 to 32 minutes or until golden brown.

Use holiday leftovers to create these tasty appetizer treats.

Dixie Caviar Cups

MAKES: 15 servings ❋ **HANDS-ON TIME:** 15 min.
TOTAL TIME: 15 min., plus 1 day for chilling

1	(15-oz.) can black-eyed peas, rinsed and drained	2	green onions, sliced
1	cup frozen whole kernel corn	1	jalapeño pepper, seeded and minced*
1	medium-size plum tomato, seeded and finely chopped	1	garlic clove, minced
		½	cup Italian dressing
½	medium-size green bell pepper, finely chopped	2	Tbsp. chopped fresh cilantro
		30	Belgian endive leaves (about 3 bunches)
½	small sweet onion, finely chopped	½	cup sour cream

1. Combine first 9 ingredients in a large zip-top plastic freezer bag. Seal bag, and chill 24 hours; drain.
2. Spoon mixture into a bowl; stir in cilantro. Spoon about 1 rounded Tbsp. mixture into each endive leaf. Dollop with sour cream.

*2¼ tsp. finely chopped pickled jalapeño peppers may be substituted.

Note: We tested with Bush's Blackeye Peas.

Three-Cheese Blackberry Quesadillas with Pepper-Peach Salsa

MAKES: 4 servings ❋ **HANDS-ON TIME:** 28 min. ❋ **TOTAL TIME:** 45 min., including peach salsa

1 (4-oz.) goat cheese log, softened	8 (7-inch) soft taco-size flour tortillas
½ (8-oz.) package cream cheese, softened	1⅔ cups fresh blackberries, halved
½ cup freshly grated Parmesan cheese	Pepper-Peach Salsa

1. Stir together softened goat cheese, softened cream cheese, and Parmesan cheese until blended. Spread cheese mixture on 1 side of each tortilla; top with blackberries. Fold in half.

2. Cook tortillas, in batches, in a lightly greased large nonstick skillet over medium-high heat 1 to 2 minutes on each side or until golden brown. Cut into wedges, and serve with Pepper-Peach Salsa.

TRY THIS TWIST!

Two-Cheese Blackberry Quesadillas: Omit goat cheese. Increase cream cheese to 1 (8-oz.) package. Proceed with recipe as directed.

Pepper-Peach Salsa

MAKES: about 1½ cups ❋ **HANDS-ON TIME:** 15 min. ❋ **TOTAL TIME:** 18 min.

2 large fresh peaches, diced (about 1½ cups)	1 tsp. lime zest
	2 tsp. fresh lime juice
½ cup peach jam	½ tsp. dried crushed red pepper

1. Stir together all ingredients in a small saucepan and cook over medium heat, stirring often, 2 to 3 minutes or until thoroughly heated.

Andouille with Smoked Paprika and Red Wine

MAKES: 8 servings ∗ **HANDS-ON TIME:** 20 min. ∗ **TOTAL TIME:** 20 min.

If you don't have smoked paprika, substitute ½ tsp. traditional paprika and ¼ tsp. ground cumin.

1 lb. andouille sausage, cut into ½-inch rounds*	2 tsp. minced garlic
2 Tbsp. olive oil	¾ tsp. smoked paprika
1 Tbsp. chopped fresh oregano	½ cup dry red wine
	Garnish: fresh oregano sprigs

1. Cook andouille sausage rounds in hot oil in a large skillet over medium-high heat 3 minutes on each side or until browned.

2. Stir in oregano, garlic, and paprika, and cook 1 minute or until fragrant. Add red wine, and cook, stirring often, 2 to 3 minutes or until wine is reduced and thickened. Transfer to a shallow bowl, and garnish, if desired. Serve with wooden picks.

*Spicy smoked sausage may be substituted.

Goat Cheese-Pesto Crostini

MAKES: about 6 to 8 servings ∗ **HANDS-ON TIME:** 20 min. ∗ **TOTAL TIME:** 30 min.

1 (8.5-oz.) French bread baguette	⅓ cup sun-dried tomatoes, drained and cut into thin strips
½ cup refrigerated pesto	
½ (10.5-oz.) package fresh goat cheese	7 pitted whole green olives, sliced

1. Preheat oven to 375°. Cut baguette into 28 (½-inch-thick) slices, and place on a lightly greased baking sheet. Bake for 5 minutes.

2. Spread 1 side of each bread slice with a layer of pesto and goat cheese. Top half of bread slices with sun-dried tomato strips and remaining half with sliced olives.

3. Bake at 375° for 5 minutes.

Andouille with Smoked
Paprika and Red Wine

Entrées for the Feast

Center your meal around one of these festive and hearty main dishes.

Grilled Filet Mignon
with Basil-Macadamia Sauce

MAKES: 4 servings ✳ **HANDS-ON TIME:** 5 min. ✳ **TOTAL TIME:** 18 min.

We cook our tenderloin fillets to medium rare. If you like your meat cooked medium or well done, increase the grilling or pan-searing time per side. (Cook approximately 1 minute more on each side for medium, 2 minutes more on each side for medium well, and 3 minutes more on each side for well done.)

4	(6-oz.) beef tenderloin fillets	½	tsp. kosher salt
1	tsp. cracked pepper		Basil-Macadamia Sauce

1. Preheat grill to 350° to 400° (medium-high) heat. Sprinkle fillets with cracked pepper and salt.
2. Grill, covered with grill lid, 4 to 6 minutes on each side or to desired degree of doneness. Let stand 5 minutes. Serve with Basil-Macadamia Sauce.

Basil-Macadamia Sauce

MAKES: 1½ cups ✳ **HANDS-ON TIME:** 10 min. ✳ **TOTAL TIME:** 10 min.

1½	cups loosely packed fresh basil leaves	¾	cup freshly grated Parmesan cheese
½	cup salted macadamia nuts	½	tsp. salt
4	large garlic cloves, minced	¼	tsp. pepper
¾	cup extra virgin olive oil		

1. Process first 3 ingredients in a food processor 3 minutes or until smooth, stopping to scrape down sides as needed. With processor running, pour oil through food chute in a slow, steady stream. Add cheese, salt, and pepper, and process 2 seconds or until smooth. Cover and chill up to 2 days.

Pan-Seared Filet Mignon

MAKES: 4 servings ❋ **HANDS-ON TIME:** 10 min. ❋ **TOTAL TIME:** 25 min.

4 (6-oz.) beef tenderloin fillets
1 tsp. cracked pepper
½ tsp. kosher salt

2 Tbsp. butter
2 Tbsp. olive oil

1. Sprinkle fillets with pepper and salt.

2. Melt butter with olive oil in a large stainless steel or cast-iron skillet over medium heat. Add fillets, and cook 5 to 7 minutes on each side or to desired degree of doneness. Let stand 5 minutes.

Balsamic-Fig Sauce

MAKES: 1 cup ＊ **HANDS-ON TIME:** 10 min. ＊ **TOTAL TIME:** 17 min.

Use aged balsamic vinegar, as regular balsamic tastes too sharp and pungent.

1 cup aged balsamic vinegar	½ tsp. kosher salt
⅓ cup fig preserves	½ tsp. freshly ground pepper
⅓ cup port	1 tsp. cognac (optional)

1. Bring first 5 ingredients to a boil in a saucepan over medium-high heat; reduce heat to medium, and simmer 6 to 7 minutes or until mixture is reduced by half. Remove from heat; stir in cognac, if desired. Serve warm.

Note: We tested with Alessi 20 Year Old Balsamic Vinegar Aged in Wood.

Creamy Horseradish Sauce

MAKES: about ¼ cup ＊ **HANDS-ON TIME:** 10 min. ＊ **TOTAL TIME:** 10 min.

¼ cup reduced-fat sour cream	1 tsp. Dijon mustard
1½ tsp. horseradish	

1. Stir together all ingredients. Serve immediately, or cover and chill up to 3 hours.

Peppered Beef Tenderloin
with Portobello-Marsala Sauce

MAKES: 6 to 8 servings ✳ **HANDS-ON TIME:** 15 min. ✳ **TOTAL TIME:** 2 hr., 33 min., including sauce

2	tsp. freshly ground black pepper	¼	tsp. dried thyme
1	tsp. kosher salt	1	(4-lb.) beef tenderloin, trimmed
1	tsp. lemon pepper		Portobello-Marsala Sauce
¼	tsp. granulated garlic		Garnish: fresh thyme sprigs

1. Combine first 5 ingredients; pat mixture evenly over beef. Cover and let stand at room temperature 30 minutes.

2. Broil 6 inches from heat 15 minutes on a lightly greased rack in a roasting pan; reduce oven temperature to 375°, and bake 30 to 35 minutes or until a meat thermometer inserted into thickest portion registers 140° or to desired degree of doneness. Remove from oven; let stand 10 minutes before slicing. Serve with Portobello-Marsala Sauce. Garnish, if desired.

Portobello-Marsala Sauce

MAKES: 1½ cups ✳ **HANDS-ON TIME:** 20 min. ✳ **TOTAL TIME:** 40 min.

3	Tbsp. cold butter, divided	2	large shallots, diced
1	(8-oz.) package sliced baby portobello mushrooms*	2	cups Marsala
		1	cup chicken broth
3	garlic cloves, minced		

1. Melt 1 Tbsp. butter in a medium skillet over high heat; add mushrooms, and sauté 10 minutes or until mushrooms are browned and liquid evaporates.

2. Add 1 Tbsp. butter, garlic, and shallots to skillet; sauté 5 minutes. Stir in Marsala and chicken broth, stirring to loosen browned bits from bottom of skillet. Bring to a boil, and cook 20 minutes or until reduced by two-thirds. Remove from heat, and stir in remaining 1 Tbsp. butter.

*1 (8-oz.) package sliced button mushrooms may be substituted.

Roasted Lamb

Roasted Lamb

MAKES: 8 servings ❋ **HANDS-ON TIME:** 20 min. ❋ **TOTAL TIME:** 2 hr., 30 min.

1 (5-lb.) boneless leg of lamb
2 lemons, halved and divided
¼ cup chopped fresh oregano
2½ tsp. salt
2 tsp. pepper
Kitchen string

1 garlic bulb, unpeeled
¼ cup olive oil
1 cup low-sodium chicken broth
Garnishes: roasted garlic cloves, baby carrots, radishes, lettuce leaves

1. Preheat oven to 350°. Unroll lamb, if necessary. Rub 1 lemon half on all sides of lamb, squeezing juice from lemon. Stir together oregano, salt, and pepper; rub on lamb. Roll up lamb, and tie with kitchen string.
2. Place lamb on a lightly greased rack in a roasting pan. Separate garlic cloves (do not peel), and place around roast. Drizzle olive oil over lamb and garlic cloves.
3. Squeeze juice from remaining 1½ lemons into a bowl. Stir together juice and chicken broth; pour into roasting pan.
4. Bake at 350° for 2 hours to 2 hours and 15 minutes or until a meat thermometer inserted into thickest portion registers 140° (medium) or to desired degree of doneness. Remove lamb from pan; cover with aluminum foil, and let stand 10 minutes before slicing. Garnish, if desired.

TRY THIS TWIST!

Roasted Boston Butt: Substitute 1 (5-lb.) bone-in pork shoulder roast (Boston butt) for lamb. Rub lemon and oregano mixture over roast as directed. (Do not tie up roast.) Proceed as directed, increasing bake time to 3 to 3½ hours or until fork-tender. Shred pork into large pieces using two forks, if desired.

For savory Greek flavor, rub a lamb roast with lemon, oregano, salt, and pepper; place garlic cloves around the roast, and drizzle with olive oil.

Rosemary Roast Lamb

MAKES: 6 to 8 servings ✳ **HANDS-ON TIME:** 20 min. ✳ **TOTAL TIME:** 4 hr., 20 min.

Serve with Roasted Carrots on page 175.

¼ cup olive oil	1 Tbsp. lemon juice
2½ Tbsp. chopped fresh rosemary	1 (5- to 6-lb.) bone-in leg of lamb
6 garlic cloves, minced	2 tsp. salt
1 Tbsp. anchovy paste	¾ tsp. pepper
1 tsp. lemon zest	

1. Combine first 6 ingredients in a small bowl.

2. Pat lamb dry, and place, fat side up, on a rack in a roasting pan. Make several 1-inch-deep slits in lamb with a paring knife; rub olive oil mixture over lamb, pressing mixture into slits. Cover loosely with aluminum foil, and let stand at room temperature 30 minutes.

3. Meanwhile, preheat oven to 400°. Uncover lamb, and sprinkle with salt and pepper.

4. Bake at 400° for 2 hours and 30 minutes or until a meat thermometer inserted into thickest portion registers 145° (medium rare). Let stand 30 minutes before slicing.

Pesto-Crusted Pork Chops with Sweet-and-Sour Collards

MAKES: 5 servings ✳ **HANDS-ON TIME:** 30 min. ✳ **TOTAL TIME:** 42 min.

½ cup golden raisins	½ cup chopped sweet onion
1 cup hot water	1 garlic clove, minced
6 (1-inch-thick) boneless pork chops (about 2 lb.)	1 (16-oz.) package frozen chopped collard greens
1 (7-oz.) container reduced-fat pesto, divided	¼ cup balsamic vinegar
1 cup panko (Japanese breadcrumbs)	1 Tbsp. brown sugar
	1 tsp. salt
6 Tbsp. olive oil, divided	½ tsp. dried crushed red pepper
	⅓ cup pine nuts, toasted

1. Stir together first 2 ingredients. Let stand 12 to 15 minutes; drain.

2. Coat pork chops with half of pesto; dredge in panko, pressing gently to adhere. Cook in ¼ cup hot oil in a large nonstick skillet over medium heat 6 to 7 minutes on each side or to desired degree of doneness.

3. Heat remaining 2 Tbsp. olive oil in skillet; add onion and garlic, and sauté 3 to 4 minutes or until tender. Add collards, and cook 3 to 4 minutes or until tender. Stir together vinegar and next 3 ingredients; add to collards, and cook 2 minutes. Remove from heat. Stir in raisins and pine nuts.

4. Serve pork chops with collards and remaining pesto.

Rosemary Roast
Lamb

Roasted Pork with
Dried Fruit and Port Sauce

MAKES: 8 servings ✳ **HANDS-ON TIME:** 21 min. ✳ **TOTAL TIME:** 49 min.

3   lb. pork tenderloin
1   tsp. salt
½   tsp. pepper
7   tsp. olive oil, divided
1   cup dried apricots
1   cup dried pitted plums
1   cup dried peaches

½   cup dried tart cherries
¼   cup pine nuts
1   cup port wine
1   cup pomegranate juice
2   (2½-inch) cinnamon sticks
½   cup chicken broth

1. Preheat oven to 425°. Remove silver skin from tenderloin, leaving a thin layer of fat. Sprinkle pork with salt and pepper. Cook pork in 6 tsp. hot oil in a large skillet over medium-high heat 3 minutes on each side or until golden brown. Transfer pork to a lightly greased jelly-roll or roasting pan, reserving drippings in skillet.

2. Bake pork at 425° for 18 to 20 minutes or until a meat thermometer inserted into thickest portion registers 150°. Remove from oven; cover and let stand 10 minutes or until thermometer registers 155°.

3. Meanwhile, add remaining 1 tsp. oil to hot drippings in skillet. Add apricots and next 4 ingredients, and sauté over medium-high heat 3 minutes or until pine nuts are toasted and fragrant. Add port wine and next 2 ingredients. Bring to a boil; reduce heat to low, and simmer 5 minutes or until mixture slightly thickens. Stir in broth, and simmer 15 minutes or until fruit is tender. Serve with pork.

Cinnamon sticks add subtle spice to this dish. Its taste and presentation are sure to impress your company.

Sage-and-Pecan Pork Tenderloin Cutlets

MAKES: 4 servings ＊ **HANDS-ON TIME:** 35 min. ＊ **TOTAL TIME:** 51 min.

1 cup red wine vinegar	2 tsp. rubbed sage
5 Tbsp. seedless blackberry preserves	2 large eggs, beaten
½ tsp. salt	4 tsp. olive oil
1 lb. pork tenderloin	Garnishes: fresh blackberries, fresh sage
¾ cup fine, dry breadcrumbs	leaves
½ cup finely chopped pecans	

1. Bring vinegar to a boil in a small saucepan over medium-high heat. Reduce heat to medium, and cook 6 minutes or until reduced by half. Stir in preserves, and cook 5 minutes. Stir in salt.

2. Remove silver skin from tenderloin, leaving a thin layer of fat covering meat. Cut pork into 8 slices. Place pork between 2 sheets of plastic wrap, and flatten to ¼-inch thickness, using a rolling pin or flat side of a meat mallet.

3. Stir together breadcrumbs, pecans, and sage in a shallow bowl.

4. Dredge pork in breadcrumb mixture, dip in beaten eggs, and dredge again in breadcrumb mixture.

5. Cook 4 pork slices in 2 tsp. hot oil in a large nonstick skillet over medium heat 8 minutes or to desired degree of doneness, turning every 2 minutes. Repeat procedure with remaining pork and oil. Serve with vinegar mixture, and garnish, if desired.

Note: It's important to turn the cutlets every 2 minutes for even browning.

test kitchen tip: preparing pork tenderloin

■ Use a sharp boning knife to strip the tough silver skin from pork tenderloin before cooking. Leaving it on can cause the tenderloin to toughen and lose shape during cooking.

Bourbon-Brown Sugar Pork Tenderloin

Bourbon-Brown Sugar Pork Tenderloin

MAKES: 6 to 8 servings ✳ **HANDS-ON TIME:** 30 min. ✳ **TOTAL TIME:** 8 hr., 30 min.

2	(1-lb.) pork tenderloins	¼	cup soy sauce
¼	cup firmly packed dark brown sugar	¼	cup Dijon mustard
¼	cup minced green onions	½	tsp. freshly ground pepper
¼	cup bourbon	½	tsp. cornstarch

1. Remove silver skin from tenderloins, leaving a thin layer of fat. Combine brown sugar and next 5 ingredients in a large zip-top plastic freezer bag; add pork. Seal bag, and chill 8 to 18 hours, turning bag occasionally. Remove pork from marinade, reserving marinade.

2. Preheat grill to 350° to 400° (medium-high) heat. Grill pork, covered with grill lid, 8 minutes on each side or until a meat thermometer inserted into thickest portion registers 155°. Remove from grill, and let stand 10 minutes.

3. Meanwhile, combine reserved marinade and cornstarch in a saucepan. Bring to a boil over medium heat; cook, stirring constantly, 1 minute. Cut pork diagonally into thin slices, and arrange on a serving platter; drizzle with warm sauce.

*1½ lb. flank steak may be substituted. Reduce grill time to 6 to 8 minutes on each side or to desired degree of doneness.

Caribbean Pork with Butter Pea Toss

MAKES: 4 servings ✳ **HANDS-ON TIME:** 15 min. ✳ **TOTAL TIME:** 45 min.

1	lb. pork tenderloin	1	tsp. fresh thyme leaves
3	Tbsp. olive oil, divided	¼	cup fresh lemon juice
1½	tsp. salt, divided	1	Tbsp. sugar
1	Tbsp. Caribbean jerk seasoning	½	tsp. dried crushed red pepper
3	cups fresh or frozen butter peas	¼	tsp. ground black pepper
¼	cup chopped fresh parsley		

1. Preheat grill to 350° to 400° (medium-high) heat. Remove silver skin from tenderloin, leaving a thin layer of fat. Rub 1 Tbsp. olive oil, ½ tsp. salt, and Caribbean seasoning over tenderloin.

2. Grill tenderloin, covered with grill lid, 10 to 12 minutes on each side or until a meat thermometer inserted into thickest portion registers 155°. Remove from grill, and let stand 5 minutes before slicing.

3. Meanwhile, bring butter peas and water to cover to a boil in a 3-qt. saucepan over high heat; reduce heat to medium, and simmer 25 minutes; drain. Combine peas, next 6 ingredients, and remaining 2 Tbsp. olive oil and 1 tsp. salt. Serve with sliced pork.

Sweet-Hot Cherry-Glazed Ham

MAKES: 10 servings ✻ **HANDS-ON TIME:** 30 min. ✻ **TOTAL TIME:** 4 hr.

Hams, especially those with a sugary glaze, need to be cooked on the lowest oven rack position and shielded with aluminum foil to prevent burning.

1	cup cherry preserves	2	tsp. minced fresh ginger
½	cup orange juice	½	tsp. dried crushed red pepper
2	Tbsp. lime juice	1	(7-lb.) smoked fully cooked,
1	Tbsp. yellow mustard		bone-in ham
1	Tbsp. honey		Garnishes: red grapes, fresh sage sprigs

1. Preheat oven to 350°. Stir together first 7 ingredients in a saucepan over medium-high heat; bring to a boil, stirring constantly. Reduce heat to medium-low; simmer, stirring constantly, 5 minutes or until preserves melt and mixture is blended. Pour half of cherry preserves mixture into a microwave-safe bowl.

2. Trim excess fat on ham to ⅛-inch thickness. If desired, make long, shallow cuts (about ¹⁄₁₆-inch deep) over entire ham, forming diamond patterns. Place ham on a rack in an aluminum foil-lined roasting pan. Brush ham with a portion of cherry preserves mixture in saucepan.

3. Bake ham at 350° on lower oven rack 1 hour and 30 minutes, basting with remaining cherry preserves mixture in saucepan every 30 minutes. Cover loosely with foil, and bake 1 hour and 45 minutes or until a meat thermometer inserted into thickest portion registers 140°, basting every 30 minutes. Let ham stand 15 minutes before slicing.

4. Microwave reserved half of cherry preserves mixture in bowl at HIGH 1 minute or until thoroughly heated. Serve ham with warm cherry preserves mixture. Garnish, if desired.

Sweet Mustard-Baked Ham

MAKES: 8 to 10 servings ❄ **HANDS-ON TIME:** 20 min. ❄ **TOTAL TIME:** 3 hr., 40 min.

Choose the size ham that best suits your family. Bake it 20 minutes per pound and 20 minutes more after you add the second layer of glaze.

1	(8-lb.) smoked, ready-to-cook, bone-in ham	2	Tbsp. cola soft drink
1	cup firmly packed light brown sugar	1	Tbsp. yellow mustard
			Garnish: fresh sage sprigs

1. Preheat oven to 350°. If necessary, trim skin or excess fat from ham. Stir together brown sugar and next 2 ingredients in a small bowl. Brush half of glaze over ham. Wrap ham tightly with heavy-duty aluminum foil. Place in a foil-lined 13- x 9-inch pan.

2. Bake ham at 350° for 2 hours and 40 minutes or until a meat thermometer inserted into ham registers 148°. Uncover ham, and brush with remaining glaze. Bake, uncovered, 20 to 30 minutes or until lightly browned. Transfer to a serving dish; let stand 20 minutes. Skim fat from pan drippings, and serve with ham. Garnish, if desired.

test kitchen tips: ham 101

■ Ham comes from the leg of the hog. You can buy it cooked, uncooked, dry cured, or wet cured.

■ A cooked ham can be served directly from the refrigerator. If you'd like to serve it hot, heat it in a 350° oven to an internal temperature of 140°. At 140°, the ham will be thoroughly warmed and moist.

■ An uncooked ham should be heated to an internal temperature of 160° in a 350° oven. Depending on the size, plan to cook it 18 to 25 minutes per pound.

■ Dry-cured hams are rubbed with salt, sugar, and other seasonings and then stored until the salt penetrates the meat.

■ Wet-cured hams are seasoned with a brine solution, which keeps the meat moist and produces a more tender texture.

Easy Roasted Chicken

MAKES: 8 servings ✸ **HANDS-ON TIME:** 10 min. ✸ **TOTAL TIME:** 1 hr., 50 min.

4 tsp. kosher salt
2 tsp. freshly ground pepper
2 (4- to 5-lb.) whole chickens

1 Tbsp. olive oil
Garnish: parsley sprigs, rosemary sprigs, lemon slices

1. Preheat oven to 375°. Stir together salt and pepper.
2. If applicable, remove necks and giblets from chickens, and reserve for another use. Pat chickens dry. Sprinkle ½ tsp. salt mixture inside cavity of each chicken. Rub 1½ tsp. olive oil into skin of each chicken. Sprinkle with remaining salt mixture; rub into skin. Place chickens, breast sides up, facing in opposite directions (for even browning), on a lightly greased wire rack in a lightly greased 17- x 12-inch jelly-roll pan.
3. Bake at 375° for 1½ hours or until a meat thermometer inserted in thigh registers 180°. Let stand 10 minutes before slicing. Garnish, if desired.

Stove-top Chicken

MAKES 4 servings ✸ **HANDS-ON TIME:** 10 min. ✸ **TOTAL TIME:** 1 hr., 15 min.

1 (4- to 5-lb.) whole chicken
1½ tsp. salt
¼ tsp. garlic powder
¼ tsp. pepper

2 Tbsp. butter
2 Tbsp. olive oil
¼ cup dry white wine

1. If applicable, remove neck and giblets from chicken, and reserve for another use. Sprinkle chicken with salt, garlic powder, and pepper.
2. Melt butter with oil in a Dutch oven over medium-high heat; add chicken, and cook, breast side down, 5 minutes or until golden brown. Turn chicken, breast side up, and reduce heat to medium-low. Add ¼ cup water and ¼ cup wine to Dutch oven. Cover and cook 1 hour or until a meat thermometer inserted in thigh registers 180°.

Easy Roasted
Chicken

Chicken Marsala

MAKES: 4 servings ❋ **HANDS-ON TIME:** 40 min. ❋ **TOTAL TIME:** 45 min.

3 Tbsp. butter, divided
1 cup pecan pieces, divided
⅓ cup all-purpose flour
4 skinned and boned chicken breasts
(about 1½ lb.)
1 tsp. salt
½ tsp. pepper
2 Tbsp. olive oil

8 oz. assorted mushrooms, trimmed
and sliced
2 shallots, sliced
¾ cup chicken broth
½ cup Marsala
¼ cup coarsely chopped fresh flat-leaf
parsley

1. Melt 1 Tbsp. butter in a small nonstick skillet over medium-low heat; add ⅔ cup pecans, and cook, stirring often, 4 to 5 minutes or until toasted and fragrant.

2. Process flour and remaining ⅓ cup pecans in a food processor until finely ground; place flour mixture in a large shallow bowl.

3. Place chicken between 2 sheets of heavy-duty plastic wrap; flatten to ¼-inch thickness, using a rolling pin or flat side of a meat mallet. Sprinkle chicken with salt and pepper; lightly dredge in flour mixture.

4. Melt remaining 2 tablespoons butter with olive oil in a large nonstick skillet over medium-high heat; add chicken, and cook 2 to 3 minutes on each side or until golden brown and done. Remove chicken from skillet.

5. Add mushrooms and shallots to skillet; sauté 3 minutes or until mushrooms are tender. Add broth and Marsala to skillet, stirring to loosen particles from bottom of skillet. Bring mixture to a boil, reduce heat to medium, and cook, stirring occasionally, 5 minutes or until sauce is slightly thickened. Return chicken to skillet, and cook 1 to 2 minutes or until thoroughly heated.

6. Transfer chicken to a serving platter; spoon mushroom-Marsala mixture over chicken, and sprinkle with parsley and toasted pecans.

Cornish Game Hens with Butternut Croutons

MAKES: 6 servings ❋ **HANDS-ON TIME:** 30 min. ❋ **TOTAL TIME:** 2 hr., 25 min., including croutons

Generally, 1-lb. hens are the perfect single-serving size. In this recipe, all six birds can be cooked on a baking sheet. Serve the dish family style (on a large platter), or plate hens individually. Either way, be sure to warm your serving dishes in advance.

Wooden picks
6   (1- to 1½-lb.) Cornish hens, rinsed and patted dry
4½   tsp. salt, divided
2   tsp. freshly ground pepper, divided

2   clementines, unpeeled and quartered
6   fresh sage leaves
Kitchen string
3   Tbsp. butter, softened
Butternut Croutons, warm

1. Preheat oven to 450°. Soak wooden picks in water to cover 30 minutes.

2. Meanwhile, season each hen cavity with ½ tsp. salt and ¼ tsp. pepper, and insert 1 clementine quarter.

3. Loosen and lift skin from hen breasts with fingers, without totally detaching skin. Place 1 sage leaf under skin of each hen. Carefully replace skin, and secure using wooden picks. Tie ends of legs together with string; tuck wingtips under.

4. Arrange hens, tail to tail in 2 rows, on a jelly-roll pan. Rub hens with butter, and sprinkle with remaining 1½ tsp. salt and ½ tsp. pepper.

5. Bake at 450° for 45 to 50 minutes or until golden brown and a meat thermometer inserted into thickest portion of thigh registers 165°. Transfer hens to a serving platter, and cover loosely with heavy-duty aluminum foil. Let stand 5 minutes before serving. Serve with warm Butternut Croutons.

Butternut Croutons

MAKES: 6 servings ❋ **HANDS-ON TIME:** 35 min. ❋ **TOTAL TIME:** 1 hr., 5 min.

3   cups (¾-inch) cubed fresh peasant-style bread
1½   lb. butternut squash, peeled and cut into ½-inch pieces (about 4 cups)
10   shallots, quartered (about 9 to 10 oz.)

1½   Tbsp. dark brown sugar
3   Tbsp. olive oil
1½   tsp. salt
¾   tsp. freshly ground white pepper
2   Tbsp. chopped fresh sage

1. Preheat oven to 400°. Bake bread cubes on a baking sheet 10 to 12 minutes or until lightly browned and toasted; cool. Increase oven temperature to 450°.

2. Mound squash and shallots in center of a lightly greased jelly-roll pan. Whisk together sugar and next 3 ingredients in a small bowl. Pour over squash and shallots, and toss to coat. Spread vegetables in a single layer in jelly-roll pan, using 2 pans if necessary.

3. Bake at 450° for 20 minutes or until tender, stirring halfway through. Toss warm squash mixture with croutons and sage in a bowl.

Delta Roasted Turkey with Million-Dollar Gravy

MAKES: 8 to 10 servings ✳ **HANDS-ON TIME:** 45 min. ✳ **TOTAL TIME:** 4 hr., 50 min.

Cheesecloth
3½ cups low-sodium fat-free chicken broth, divided
5 thick hickory-smoked bacon slices
½ cup butter, softened
2 tsp. salt
2 tsp. pepper
1 (14-lb.) whole fresh or frozen turkey, thawed
Kitchen string

2 cups dry white wine
2 bay leaves
6 black peppercorns
4 fresh thyme sprigs
4 fresh parsley sprigs
1 cup butter
3 Tbsp. all-purpose flour
2 Tbsp. butter, softened
Garnishes: lemon halves and slices, fresh bay leaves, beet greens

1. Cut cheesecloth into a 3- x 3-ft. square. (Cheesecloth should be large enough to wrap around entire turkey.) Soak cheesecloth in 1 cup broth 15 minutes. Wring out cheesecloth, discarding excess broth. Lay cheesecloth on top of a roasting rack in a roasting pan. Place bacon in center of cheesecloth.

2. Preheat oven to 500°. Combine ½ cup softened butter, salt, and pepper. Remove giblets and neck from turkey, and pat turkey dry with paper towels. Loosen and lift skin from turkey breast with fingers, without totally detaching skin; rub about one-third of butter mixture underneath skin. Carefully replace skin, and rub remaining butter mixture over outside of turkey. Tie ends of legs together with kitchen string; tuck wingtips under. Place turkey, breast side down, on top of bacon in roasting pan. Lift sides of cheesecloth up and over turkey. Twist ends of cheesecloth together, and secure tightly with string. Trim excess cheesecloth and string.

3. Stir together wine, next 4 ingredients, and 1 cup broth. Pour into roasting pan.

4. Bake turkey at 500° for 30 minutes.

5. Meanwhile, heat 1 cup butter and ½ cup broth in a saucepan over low heat just until butter is melted. Pour mixture over turkey. Reduce oven temperature to 300°, and bake 2½ hours, basting with pan drippings every 30 minutes.

6. Remove turkey from oven, and increase oven temperature to 400°. Carefully transfer turkey to a cutting board, using clean dish towels. Remove and discard cheesecloth and bacon. Carefully return turkey, breast side up, to roasting pan.

7. Bake turkey at 400° for 30 minutes or until skin is golden brown and a meat thermometer inserted into thickest portion of thigh registers 170° to 175°. Transfer turkey to a serving platter, reserving pan drippings in roasting pan. Let turkey stand 20 minutes before carving.

8. Pour pan drippings through a fine wire-mesh strainer into a 4-cup glass measuring cup. Let stand 10 minutes. Remove excess fat from surface of drippings.

9. Pour 2 cups drippings into a medium saucepan; stir in remaining 1 cup broth. Bring to a boil over medium-high heat. Combine flour and 2 Tbsp. butter to form a smooth paste. Whisk butter mixture into broth mixture, and cook, whisking constantly, 2 minutes or until thickened. Serve with turkey. Garnish, if desired.

test kitchen secrets

Here are a few tips for success when making Delta Roasted Turkey:

■ Carefully read our recipe before getting started. It's involved and takes some time to make, but it's definitely worth it.

■ Don't skimp on the cheesecloth—or skip it. Cut the piece large enough to cover the entire bird. Using it helps keep the bacon laying against the bird, which infuses more flavor. And it keeps the turkey super-moist.

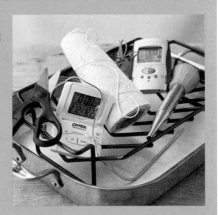

■ Use a V-shaped roasting rack to hold the turkey snuggly in place above the drippings for beautiful browning and a pretty shape. In a pinch, your favorite pan and rack will work.

Roasted Turkey with Béarnaise Butter

MAKES: 8 servings ✳ **HANDS-ON TIME:** 40 min.
TOTAL TIME: 4 hr., 50 min., including butter and roasted onions

1 (12- to 15-lb.) whole fresh turkey*
Béarnaise Butter, divided
Salt and freshly ground pepper
Kitchen string
2 cups dry white wine

2½ cups chicken broth, divided
¼ cup all-purpose flour
Garnishes: Roasted Onions, fresh herb sprigs, grapes, fresh lavender

1. Preheat oven to 325°. Remove giblets and neck from turkey, and rinse turkey with cold water. Drain cavity well; pat dry. Loosen and lift skin from turkey breast without totally detaching skin. Rub ¼ cup Béarnaise Butter under skin; replace skin. Sprinkle cavity and outside of turkey with desired amount of salt and freshly ground pepper.

2. Place turkey, breast side up, on a lightly greased roasting rack in a large roasting pan. Tie ends of legs together with string; tuck wingtips under. Rub entire turkey with ¼ cup Béarnaise Butter. Pour wine and 2 cups chicken broth into roasting pan.

3. Bake at 325° for 3 hours and 15 minutes to 4 hours or until a meat thermometer inserted into thickest portion of thigh registers 165°, basting every 30 minutes with pan juices. Shield with aluminum foil after 1½ hours to prevent excessive browning, if necessary. Remove from oven, and let stand 30 minutes.

4. Transfer turkey to a serving platter, reserving 2½ cups pan drippings. Pour reserved drippings through a fine wire-mesh strainer into a bowl, discarding solids.

5. Melt remaining Béarnaise Butter in a saucepan over medium heat; whisk in flour, and cook, whisking constantly, 1 to 2 minutes or until smooth. Gradually add reserved drippings to saucepan, and bring to a boil, whisking constantly. Reduce heat, and simmer, stirring occasionally, 5 minutes or until thickened. Add up to ½ cup remaining chicken broth for desired consistency. Add salt and pepper to taste. Serve turkey with gravy. Garnish, if desired.

*Frozen whole turkey, thawed, may be substituted.

Béarnaise Butter

MAKES: about 1 cup ❋ **HANDS-ON TIME:** 15 min. ❋ **TOTAL TIME:** 25 min.

⅓ cup dry white wine	1 Tbsp. chopped fresh tarragon
1 Tbsp. white wine vinegar	1 tsp. lemon zest
2 shallots, minced (about ¼ cup)	⅛ tsp. pepper
¾ cup butter, softened	

1. Cook first 3 ingredients in a small saucepan over medium-high heat 5 minutes or until liquid is reduced to 1 Tbsp. Remove from heat, and cool 10 minutes. Stir in butter and remaining ingredients. Store in an airtight container in refrigerator up to 5 days.

Roasted Onions

MAKES: 8 to 10 servings ❋ **HANDS-ON TIME:** 45 min. ❋ **TOTAL TIME:** 1hr., 15 min.

¼ cup firmly packed light brown sugar	4 small red onions, quartered
¼ cup olive oil	1 lb. pearl onions
¼ cup balsamic vinegar	1 lb. cipollini onions
½ tsp. salt	1 lb. shallots

1. Preheat oven to 450°. Whisk together first 4 ingredients in a large bowl.

2. Toss red onions and next 3 ingredients with oil mixture. Arrange in a single layer on a lightly greased 17- x 12-inch jelly-roll pan. Bake at 450° for 30 to 40 minutes or until tender and golden brown, stirring twice.

Casual Entrées

*Put together the perfect
holiday dinner with these dishes.*

Chilled Carrot Soup

MAKES: 5 cups ❋ **HANDS-ON TIME:** 30 min. ❋ **TOTAL TIME:** 6 hr., 5 min.

Serve this tasty soup with bacon at a holiday brunch.

3	cups peeled and diced baking potatoes
2	cups diced carrots
1½	cups chopped leeks
1	(32-oz.) container chicken broth
1	Tbsp. jarred chicken soup base

1	cup half-and-half
½	tsp. salt
¼	tsp. ground white pepper
Garnish: finely shredded carrots	

1. Combine first 5 ingredients in a Dutch oven; bring to a boil over medium-high heat. Cover, reduce heat to low, and simmer 10 minutes or until vegetables are tender. Cool 10 minutes.
2. Purée vegetable mixture, in batches, in a blender until smooth. Transfer purée to a large bowl; whisk in half-and-half, salt, and white pepper until blended. Cool 1 hour; cover and chill 4 to 48 hours.
3. Add salt and white pepper to taste. Serve in chilled cups. Garnish, if desired.

Note: We tested with Superior Touch Better Than Bouillon Chicken Base.

Quick Turkey Chili

MAKES: 6 to 8 servings ✳ **HANDS-ON TIME:** 31 min. ✳ **TOTAL TIME:** 1 hr., 6 min.

Don't let the long list of ingredients deter you; chances are you'll have most of them on hand already.

1 medium onion, chopped	1 (16-oz.) can kidney beans, drained
1 Tbsp. vegetable oil	and rinsed
2 garlic cloves, chopped	1 cup chicken broth
1 lb. ground turkey	1 cup beer*
2 Tbsp. chili powder	1 tsp. salt
2 tsp. ground cumin	½ tsp. pepper
3 Tbsp. tomato paste	¼ cup chopped fresh cilantro
1 (28-oz.) can diced tomatoes	Garnish: sour cream

1. Sauté chopped onion in hot oil in a large Dutch oven over medium-high heat 5 minutes or until tender; add garlic, and sauté 1 minute.

2. Add turkey, chili powder, and cumin, and cook, stirring often, 8 minutes or until meat crumbles and is no longer pink. Stir in tomato paste, and cook 2 minutes. Add tomatoes and next 5 ingredients. Bring mixture to a boil; cover, reduce heat to low, and simmer, stirring occasionally, 30 minutes. Stir in chopped cilantro. Garnish, if desired.

*Chicken broth may be substituted.

Tomato-and-Corn Pizza

Tomato-and-Corn Pizza

MAKES: 4 servings ❋ **HANDS-ON TIME:** 10 min. ❋ **TOTAL TIME:** 44 min.

3 small plum tomatoes, sliced	⅓ cup refrigerated pesto
¼ tsp. salt	½ cup fresh corn kernels
⅛ tsp. freshly ground pepper	¼ cup grated Parmesan cheese
1 (14-oz.) package prebaked Italian pizza crust	1 tsp. sugar
	8 oz. fresh mozzarella, sliced
Parchment paper	3 Tbsp. fresh whole or torn basil leaves

1. Preheat oven to 450°. Place tomato slices on paper towels. Sprinkle with salt and pepper; let stand 20 minutes.

2. Place pizza crust on a parchment paper-lined baking sheet; spread with pesto. Stir together corn, Parmesan, and sugar. Top pizza with corn mixture, tomatoes, and mozzarella slices.

3. Bake at 450° for 14 minutes or until cheese is melted and golden. Remove from oven, and top with basil leaves.

Note: We tested with Boboli Original Pizza Crust.

Creamy Tortellini Primavera

MAKES: 4 servings ❋ **HANDS-ON TIME:** 24 min. ❋ **TOTAL TIME:** 35 min.

By draining and rinsing with cold water, the tortellini will not stick together while you prepare the sauce.

1 (10-oz.) package refrigerated reduced-fat Alfredo sauce	3 garlic cloves, minced
2 Tbsp. dry white wine	2 Tbsp. olive oil
¼ tsp. dried crushed red pepper	1½ cups sliced fresh mushrooms
1 lb. fresh asparagus	½ tsp. salt
1 (20-oz.) package refrigerated cheese-filled tortellini	1 cup halved grape tomatoes
	¼ cup freshly grated Parmesan cheese

1. Stir together first 3 ingredients. Snap off and discard tough ends of asparagus; cut into 1-inch pieces.

2. Bring 5 qt. salted water to a boil; add tortellini, and cook 6 minutes or just until tender. (Pasta should still be firm to bite.) Drain; rinse with cold water, and drain well again. Place in a serving bowl.

3. Sauté garlic in hot oil over medium-high heat 1 minute or until garlic is lightly browned. Stir in mushrooms, asparagus, and salt; sauté 3 to 5 minutes or until asparagus is crisp-tender. Reduce heat to medium, and stir in Alfredo sauce mixture. Cook 5 minutes or until thoroughly heated.

4. Pour sauce mixture over tortellini; toss gently. Sprinkle with tomatoes and Parmesan cheese. Serve immediately.

Note: We tested with refrigerated Buitoni Light Alfredo Sauce and Buitoni Three Cheese Tortellini.

Linguine with Sun-Dried Tomatoes

MAKES: 6 servings ∗ **HANDS-ON TIME:** 16 min. ∗ **TOTAL TIME:** 26 min.

1 (16-oz.) package linguine
1 (7-oz.) jar sun-dried tomatoes in oil
¼ cup pine nuts
3 garlic cloves, minced

¼ cup extra virgin olive oil
1 (4-oz.) package crumbled feta cheese
2 Tbsp. thin fresh basil strips

1. Prepare linguine according to package directions.

2. Drain tomatoes, reserving 2 Tbsp. oil. Cut tomatoes into thin strips.

3. Heat pine nuts in a large nonstick skillet over medium-low heat, stirring often, 5 minutes or until toasted and fragrant. Remove nuts from skillet.

4. Increase heat to medium, and sauté garlic in 2 Tbsp. reserved oil and olive oil in skillet 1 minute or until garlic is fragrant. Stir in tomatoes, and remove from heat.

5. Toss together tomato mixture, hot cooked pasta, feta cheese, and basil in a large serving bowl. Sprinkle with toasted pine nuts.

---

test kitchen tip: how to toast pine nuts in the oven

Toasting intensifies the flavor of nuts. But the nut is a mighty delicate thing in an oven—it can go from perfectly toasty to charred in seconds. This has happened to every one of our Test Kitchen cooks.

■ Arrange nuts in a single layer on a heavy baking sheet, and bake at 350° for as little as two minutes to five or more minutes; shake the pan or stir frequently so the nuts toast evenly (they tend to brown on the bottom more quickly). They're done when they've darkened slightly (or turned golden brown) and smell fragrant and toasty.

Fresh Vegetable Lasagna

MAKES: 8 servings ∗ HANDS-ON TIME: 30 min. ∗ TOTAL TIME: 3 hr., 14 min., including sauce

4	medium zucchini, halved lengthwise and thinly sliced (about 1½ lb.)
1	(8-oz.) package sliced fresh mushrooms
2	garlic cloves, minced
	Vegetable cooking spray
1	medium-size red bell pepper, chopped
1	medium-size yellow bell pepper, chopped
1	yellow onion, chopped

½	tsp. salt
1½	cups fat-free ricotta cheese
1	large egg
2	cups (8 oz.) shredded part-skim mozzarella cheese, divided
½	cup freshly grated Parmesan cheese, divided
5	cups Basic Marinara Sauce
1	(8-oz.) package no-boil lasagna noodles

1. Preheat oven to 450°. Bake zucchini, mushrooms, and garlic in a jelly-roll pan coated with cooking spray 12 to 14 minutes or until vegetables are crisp-tender, stirring halfway through. Repeat procedure with bell peppers and onion. Reduce oven temperature to 350°. Toss together vegetables and salt in a bowl.

2. Stir together ricotta, egg, 1½ cups shredded mozzarella cheese, and ¼ cup grated Parmesan cheese.

3. Spread 1 cup Basic Marinara Sauce in a 13- x 9-inch baking dish coated with cooking spray. Top with 3 noodles, 1 cup sauce, one-third of ricotta mixture, and one-third of vegetable mixture; repeat layers twice, beginning with 3 noodles. Top with remaining noodles and 1 cup sauce. Sprinkle with remaining ½ cup shredded mozzarella and ¼ cup grated Parmesan.

4. Bake, covered, at 350° for 45 minutes. Uncover and bake 10 to 15 more minutes or until cheese is melted and golden. Let stand 10 minutes.

Note: We tested with Ronzoni Oven Ready Lasagna.

Basic Marinara Sauce

MAKES: 11 cups ∗ HANDS-ON TIME: 17 min. ∗ TOTAL TIME: 1 hr., 15 min.

3	cups chopped yellow onions (about 3 medium)
3	Tbsp. olive oil
1	Tbsp. sugar
3	garlic cloves, minced
5	tsp. freshly ground Italian seasoning

2	tsp. salt
2	Tbsp. balsamic vinegar
2	cups low-sodium fat-free vegetable broth
3	(28-oz.) cans no-salt-added crushed tomatoes

1. Sauté onions in hot oil in a large Dutch oven over medium-high heat 5 minutes or until tender. Add sugar and next 3 ingredients; sauté 1 minute. Stir in vinegar; cook 30 seconds. Add broth and tomatoes. Bring to a boil; reduce heat to low, and simmer, stirring occasionally, 55 minutes or until sauce thickens.

Note: We tested with McCormick Italian Herb Seasoning Grinder (set on medium) and Dei Fratelli Crushed Tomatoes.

Ragout of Mushrooms with Creamy Polenta

MAKES: 6 servings ❋ **HANDS-ON TIME:** 28 min. ❋ **TOTAL TIME:** 40 min., including polenta

1 cup halved and thinly sliced shallots

3 garlic cloves, minced

4 Tbsp. olive oil

2 (8-oz.) packages sliced baby portobello mushrooms*

2 (3.5-oz.) packages fresh shiitake mushrooms, stemmed and sliced

½ cup port

1 cup chicken broth

4 Tbsp. fresh flat-leaf parsley leaves, chopped

4 Tbsp. butter

1½ Tbsp. fresh thyme leaves

¾ tsp. salt

½ tsp. pepper

Creamy Polenta

Freshly grated Parmesan cheese

Garnish: fresh thyme sprigs

1. Sauté shallots and garlic in hot oil in a large skillet over medium heat 2 minutes. Increase heat to medium-high. Add mushrooms, and cook, stirring constantly, 4 to 5 minutes. Stir in port; cook 2 minutes. Stir in chicken broth and next 5 ingredients. Reduce heat to low; simmer 5 minutes or until slightly thickened.
2. Serve over Creamy Polenta with grated Parmesan cheese. Garnish, if desired.

*2 (8-oz.) packages sliced fresh button mushrooms may be substituted.

Creamy Polenta

MAKES: 6 servings ❋ **HANDS-ON TIME:** 7 min. ❋ **TOTAL TIME:** 12 min.

Polenta can be found in the gourmet or international section of the grocery store. Don't let the polenta boil, or it will spatter.

7 cups chicken broth

2 cups polenta

1 (8-oz.) package ⅓-less-fat cream cheese

1. Bring 6 cups chicken broth to a light boil in a Dutch oven over medium-high heat; slowly stir in polenta. Reduce heat to low, and cook, stirring constantly, 2 to 3 minutes or until polenta thickens. (Do not boil.) Stir in cream cheese until blended. Stir in remaining broth. Cover and keep warm.

Holiday Meatloaf

MAKES: 10 servings ※ **HANDS-ON TIME:** 15 min. ※ **TOTAL TIME:** 1 hr., 50 min.

2	lb. lean ground beef		2	large eggs, lightly beaten
1	lb. ground pork sausage		1	Tbsp. Worcestershire sauce
18	saltine crackers, crushed		1	tsp. yellow mustard
½	green bell pepper, diced		½	cup firmly packed brown sugar, divided
½	onion, finely chopped		½	cup ketchup

1. Preheat oven to 350°. Combine first 8 ingredients and ¼ cup brown sugar in a medium bowl just until blended. Place mixture in a lightly greased 11- x 7-inch baking dish, and shape mixture into a 10- x 5-inch loaf.
2. Bake at 350° for 1 hour. Remove from oven, and drain. Stir together ketchup and remaining ¼ cup brown sugar; pour over meatloaf. Bake 15 more minutes or until a meat thermometer inserted into thickest portion registers 160°. Remove from oven; let stand 20 minutes. Remove from baking dish before slicing.

test kitchen tip: how to make a meatloaf

■ Use your hands to combine the ingredients in a large bowl. Shape a free-form meatloaf. Use a meat thermometer to test the loaf's doneness (160° for ground beef, pork, or veal; 165° for ground poultry). Let the loaf stand 10 minutes before slicing. Slice and serve.

Cheesy Chili
Hash Brown Bake

Cheesy Chili Hash Brown Bake

MAKES: 8 servings ✳ **HANDS-ON TIME:** 12 min. ✳ **TOTAL TIME:** 57 min.

1½   lb. lean ground beef or turkey
1   (15.5-oz.) can original Sloppy Joe sauce
1   (15-oz.) can chili with beans

½   (30-oz.) package frozen country-style shredded hash browns (about 4 cups)
2   cups (8 oz.) shredded Cheddar cheese

1. Preheat oven to 425°. Brown ground beef in a large skillet over medium-high heat, stirring often, 7 to 10 minutes or until meat crumbles and is no longer pink. Stir in Sloppy Joe sauce and chili.
2. Spoon chili mixture into 8 lightly greased 10-oz. ramekins. Top with frozen hash browns.
3. Bake, covered, at 425° for 30 minutes; uncover and bake 10 more minutes or until browned and crisp. Sprinkle with cheese, and bake 5 more minutes or until cheese is melted.

Note: We tested with Hunt's Manwich Original Sloppy Joe Sauce and Hormel Chili with Beans. Chili mixture can be baked in a lightly greased 13- x 9-inch baking dish as directed.

Tomato-Basil Meatloaf

MAKES: 6 to 8 servings ✳ **HANDS-ON TIME:** 10 min. ✳ **TOTAL TIME:** 1 hr., 30 min.

1   lb. ground chuck
1   lb. lean ground pork
1   (14.5-oz.) can diced tomatoes with basil, oregano, and garlic, drained
⅓   cup marinara sauce

⅓   cup Italian-seasoned breadcrumbs
1   large egg, lightly beaten
1   tsp. salt
1   tsp. pepper
½   cup (2 oz.) shredded mozzarella cheese

1. Preheat oven to 375°. Stir together ground chuck and pork in a large bowl.
2. Process diced tomatoes in a blender or food processor 5 seconds or until slightly chunky, stopping to scrape down sides as needed. Stir tomatoes, marinara sauce, and next 4 ingredients into ground beef mixture just until combined. Shape into a 9- x 5-inch loaf.
3. Place meatloaf on a wire rack in an aluminum foil-lined jelly-roll pan.
4. Bake at 375° for 1 hour. Top with mozzarella cheese, and bake 15 more minutes or until center is no longer pink. Let stand 5 minutes before serving.

Shepherd's Pie

MAKES: 6 to 8 servings ❋ **HANDS-ON TIME:** 50 min. ❋ **TOTAL TIME:** 2 hr., 6 min., including potatoes

1½	lb. ground round		½	tsp. dried thyme
1	cup chopped onion		¼	tsp. freshly ground pepper
½	(8-oz.) package fresh mushrooms, sliced		1	Tbsp. all-purpose flour
1	garlic clove, minced		1	(14½-oz.) can stewed tomatoes
1	cup frozen peas, thawed		1	bay leaf
4	tsp. beef bouillon granules		2	Tbsp. red wine vinegar
½	tsp. salt			Cheese-and-Carrot Mashed Potatoes

1. Preheat oven to 400°. Brown ground beef in a large nonstick skillet over medium-high heat, stirring often, 10 minutes or until meat crumbles and is no longer pink. Remove ground beef from skillet using a slotted spoon; reserve 2 Tbsp. drippings in skillet. Reduce heat to medium.

2. Sauté onion, mushrooms, and garlic in hot drippings over medium heat 10 to 11 minutes or until tender. Stir in beef, peas, and next 4 ingredients. Sprinkle flour over meat mixture. Increase heat to medium-high; cook, stirring constantly, 1 minute. Stir in tomatoes, bay leaf, and vinegar, breaking up large tomato pieces. Reduce heat to medium; cook, stirring often, 3 minutes or until slightly thickened. Remove bay leaf. Transfer mixture to a lightly greased 3-qt. baking dish or pan. Spoon Cheese-and-Carrot Mashed Potatoes over meat mixture, smoothing with back of spoon.

3. Bake at 400° for 15 minutes. Let stand 5 minutes before serving.

Cheese-and-Carrot Mashed Potatoes

MAKES: 8 servings ❋ **HANDS-ON TIME:** 20 min. ❋ **TOTAL TIME:** 28 min.

1	(1-lb.) package baby carrots		1	Tbsp. fresh thyme leaves
1	Tbsp. butter		1	tsp. salt
3	cups prepared mashed potatoes		¼	tsp. pepper
1	cup (4 oz.) Cheddar cheese			

1. Place baby carrots and ¼ cup water in a large microwave-safe bowl. Cover tightly with plastic wrap; fold back a small edge to allow steam to escape. Microwave at HIGH 8 minutes or until tender. Drain. Stir in butter. Coarsely mash carrots with a potato masher. Stir in mashed potatoes, cheese, fresh thyme leaves, salt, and pepper until blended.

Hamburger Steak with
Sweet Onion-and-Mushroom Gravy

MAKES: 4 servings ✳ **HANDS-ON TIME:** 25 min. ✳ **TOTAL TIME:** 38 min.

2	honey-wheat bread slices	1	(1.2-oz.) envelope brown gravy mix
1	lb. ground round	1	Tbsp. vegetable oil
1	large egg, lightly beaten	1	(8-oz.) package sliced fresh mushrooms
2	garlic cloves, minced	1	medium-size sweet onion, halved and
½	tsp. salt		thinly sliced
½	tsp. freshly ground pepper		

1. Process bread slices in a food processor 10 seconds or until finely chopped. Place breadcrumbs in a bowl; add ground round and next 4 ingredients. Gently combine until blended, using your hands. Shape into 4 (4-inch) patties.

2. Whisk together gravy mix and 1½ cups water.

3. Cook patties in hot oil in a large skillet over medium-high heat 2 minutes on each side or just until browned. Remove from skillet. Add mushrooms and onion to skillet, and sauté 6 minutes or until tender. Stir in prepared gravy, and bring to a light boil. Return patties to skillet, and spoon gravy over each patty. Cover, reduce heat to low, and simmer 8 to 10 minutes.

Note: This dish can be made ahead and frozen. Wrap each patty individually in plastic wrap, place in a large zip-top plastic freezer bag, and freeze up to 3 months. To reheat, thaw frozen patties in the refrigerator overnight, and proceed with steps 2 and 3.

Bacon-Wrapped Pork Tenderloin

MAKES: 4 servings ❊ **HANDS-ON TIME:** 10 min. ❊ **TOTAL TIME:** 48 min.

1   (1-lb.) pork tenderloin
1   tsp. steak seasoning

3   bacon slices, cut in half crosswise
Wooden picks

1. Preheat oven to 425°. Remove silver skin from pork tenderloin, leaving a thin layer of fat. Sprinkle seasoning over pork. Wrap pork with bacon slices, and secure with wooden picks. Place pork on a lightly greased wire rack in an aluminum foil-lined roasting pan.

2. Bake at 425° for 25 minutes or until a meat thermometer inserted into thickest portion registers 155°. Increase oven temperature to broil with oven rack 5 inches from heat. Broil 3 to 5 minutes or until bacon is crisp. Remove from oven. Cover pork with foil; let stand 10 minutes or until thermometer registers 160°.

Note: We tested with McCormick Grill Mates Montreal Steak Seasoning.

Oven-Fried Pork Chops with Roasted Green Beans and Pecans

MAKES: 4 servings ❊ **HANDS-ON TIME:** 30 min. ❊ **TOTAL TIME:** 30 min.

2   (12-oz.) packages fresh cut green beans
1   Tbsp. olive oil
1   tsp. salt, divided
4   (4- to 6-oz.) bone-in center-cut pork chops
¼   tsp. pepper

½   cup panko (Japanese breadcrumbs)
¼   cup freshly grated Parmesan cheese
1   Tbsp. lemon zest
1   tsp. chopped fresh thyme
¼   cup vegetable oil
¼   cup chopped pecans
½   Tbsp. butter

1. Preheat oven to 450°. Drain and rinse beans. Combine beans, 1 Tbsp. olive oil, and ¾ tsp. salt in a large bowl, tossing to coat. Spread beans in a single layer in a jelly-roll pan. Bake 18 to 20 minutes or until beans are tender and slightly browned.

2. Meanwhile, sprinkle pork chops with pepper and remaining ¼ tsp. salt.

3. Stir together breadcrumbs and next 3 ingredients in a large shallow dish. Dredge pork chops in breadcrumb mixture.

4. Cook chops in ¼ cup hot vegetable oil in a large skillet over medium heat 5 to 6 minutes on each side or to desired degree of doneness.

5. Meanwhile, stir pecans and butter into beans; bake at 450° 5 or 6 more minutes or until pecans are golden. Serve pork chops with green beans.

Bacon-Wrapped Pork Tenderloin

Pork Chops with Red Pepper Jelly Sauce

MAKES: 6 servings ✳ **HANDS-ON TIME:** 39 min. ✳ **TOTAL TIME:** 39 min.

4 (¾-inch-thick) bone-in pork loin chops (about 2¼ lb.)
1 tsp. salt
¾ tsp. freshly ground pepper
3 Tbsp. butter, divided
3 Tbsp. olive oil
1 Tbsp. all-purpose flour
1 large jalapeño pepper, seeded and minced
⅓ cup dry white wine
1 cup chicken broth
½ cup red pepper jelly
Salt and freshly ground pepper to taste

1. Sprinkle pork with salt and pepper. Melt 1 Tbsp. butter with oil in a 12-inch cast-iron skillet over medium-high heat. Add pork chops, and cook 8 minutes; turn and cook 10 minutes or until a meat thermometer inserted into thickest portion registers 150°. Remove from skillet, and keep warm.

2. Add flour and jalapeño to skillet. Cook, stirring constantly, 1 to 2 minutes or until flour is golden brown. Add wine, stirring to loosen particles from bottom of skillet; cook 1 minute or until liquid is almost completely reduced.

3. Add chicken broth, and cook 2 to 3 minutes or until mixture begins to thicken. Whisk in pepper jelly until melted and smooth. Cook 3 to 4 minutes or until thickened. Remove from heat. Stir in remaining 2 Tbsp. butter. Season with salt and freshly ground pepper to taste. Return pork to skillet; turn to coat. Serve pork with sauce.

Note: We tested with Braswell's Red Pepper Jelly.

Savory Herb Pork Chops

MAKES: 4 servings ✳ **HANDS-ON TIME:** 40 min. ✳ **TOTAL TIME:** 1 hr., 5 min.

1 cup apple juice, divided
3½ Tbsp. light brown sugar, divided
1 Tbsp. Dijon mustard
4 (¾-inch-thick) boneless pork loin chops
1 tsp. salt, divided
1 tsp. coarsely ground pepper, divided
2 Tbsp. vegetable oil

½ cup chopped onion
2 garlic cloves, minced
2 tsp. chopped fresh rosemary
2 Tbsp. balsamic vinegar, divided
1 Tbsp. all-purpose flour
Garnishes: thinly sliced apples, fresh rosemary sprigs

1. Stir together ¼ cup apple juice, 1 Tbsp. brown sugar, and mustard in a large zip-top plastic freezer bag; add pork. Seal bag, and shake well to coat. Chill 30 minutes, turning once. Remove pork from marinade, discarding marinade. Pat pork dry, and sprinkle with ½ tsp. salt and ½ tsp. pepper.

2. Cook pork in hot oil in large skillet over medium-high heat 3 minutes on each side. Remove chops from skillet.

3. Cook onion and garlic in hot drippings, stirring constantly, 1 minute. Add remaining ¾ cup apple juice to skillet, stirring to loosen particles from bottom of skillet. Stir in rosemary, 1 Tbsp. brown sugar, 1 Tbsp. balsamic vinegar, and remaining ½ tsp. salt and pepper.

4. Bring onion mixture to a boil. Reduce heat to medium low, and simmer 3 to 5 minutes or until mixture is reduced by half.

5. Add pork to onion mixture, turning to coat. Cover and cook 5 to 10 minutes or until a meat thermometer inserted in thickest portion registers 155°. Remove from heat, and place pork on a serving platter. Cover with aluminum foil. Let stand 5 minutes.

6. Meanwhile, whisk together ¼ cup water, flour, remaining 1½ Tbsp. brown sugar, and remaining 1 Tbsp. balsamic vinegar in skillet until smooth. Bring to a boil over medium-low heat. Reduce heat to low, and simmer 1 to 2 minutes or until slightly thickened and bubbly. Drizzle sauce over pork, or serve with pork, if desired. Garnish, if desired.

Oven-Fried Pork Chops

MAKES: 4 servings ❋ **HANDS-ON TIME:** 10 min. ❋ **TOTAL TIME:** 20 min.

4 (½-inch-thick) pork chops (about 1½ lb.)
1 tsp. salt
½ tsp. black pepper
⅛ tsp. ground red pepper

1 sleeve saltine crackers, crushed (about 1 cup crushed)
1 large egg, lightly beaten
Vegetable cooking spray

1. Preheat oven to 425°. Sprinkle pork chops evenly with salt, black pepper, and red pepper. Place cracker crumbs in a shallow dish.

2. Dip chops in egg, and dredge in cracker crumbs. Place on a lightly greased rack on a baking sheet. Spray chops evenly with cooking spray.

3. Bake at 425° for 8 to 10 minutes or to desired degree of doneness.

Spicy Tomato Sauce with Italian Sausage

MAKES: about 5¼ cups   ✳   **HANDS-ON TIME:** 25 min.   ✳   **TOTAL TIME:** 1 hr., 15 min.

Reduce amount of seasoning mix for a less-spicy sauce.

½   lb. mild Italian sausage (about 2 sausages)
½   cup finely chopped onion
2   tsp. minced garlic
1   Tbsp. extra virgin olive oil
1½   Tbsp. Italian Seasoning Mix
1   (28-oz.) can crushed tomatoes

1   (8-oz.) can Spanish-style tomato sauce
1   tsp. kosher salt
1   tsp. honey
Garnishes: fresh basil sprig, shaved Parmesan cheese

1. Remove casings from sausage, and cook in a 3-qt. saucepan over medium heat 8 to 10 minutes or until meat is no longer pink, breaking sausage into pieces. Drain; return sausage to pan.

2. Sauté onion and garlic in hot oil in saucepan over medium heat 2 to 3 minutes or until tender. Stir in Italian Seasoning Mix, and cook 1 minute. Stir in crushed tomatoes, tomato sauce, and 1 cup water; bring to a boil, stirring constantly. Reduce heat to low; simmer 40 to 45 minutes or until slightly thickened. Stir in salt and honey. Garnish, if desired.

Note: We tested with Goya Tomato Sauce.

Italian Seasoning Mix

MAKES: about ½ cup * **HANDS-ON TIME:** 5 min. * **TOTAL TIME:** 5 min.

Don't want to get out the food processor? You can use a mortar and pestle to grind these ingredients.

½ cup dried basil	4 tsp. dried crushed red pepper
2 Tbsp. plus 2 tsp. dried oregano	2 tsp. whole black peppercorns

1. Process all ingredients in a food processor 1 minute or until mixture is a fine powder. Store in an airtight container at room temperature up to 4 months.

TRY THIS TWIST!

Baked Ziti with Italian Sausage: Preheat oven to 350°. Prepare 1 (16-oz.) package ziti pasta according to package directions. Stir together pasta, Spicy Tomato Sauce with Italian Sausage, and ½ cup mozzarella cheese. Spoon mixture into a lightly greased 11- x 7-inch baking dish. Sprinkle with ½ cup mozzarella cheese. Bake at 350° for 20 to 25 minutes or until cheese melts. Let stand 10 minutes before serving. MAKES: 4 to 6 servings; HANDS-ON TIME: 10 min.; TOTAL TIME: 40 min.

Sausage-and-Ravioli Lasagna

MAKES: 6 to 8 servings * **HANDS-ON TIME:** 25 min. * **TOTAL TIME:** 1 hr.

Keep the ingredients on hand, and you'll be ready when the craving for Italian hits.

½ lb. ground Italian sausage	1 (25-oz.) package frozen cheese-filled ravioli (do not thaw)
1 (24-oz.) jar tomato-and-basil pasta sauce	
1 (6-oz.) package fresh baby spinach	1 cup (4 oz.) shredded Italian six-cheese blend
½ cup refrigerated pesto sauce	

1. Preheat oven to 375°. Cook Italian sausage in a skillet over medium heat, stirring often, 10 minutes or until sausage crumbles and is no longer pink; drain well. Stir pasta sauce into sausage.
2. Chop spinach, and toss with pesto.
3. Spoon one-third of sausage mixture (about ½ cup) into a lightly greased 11- x 7-inch baking dish. Top with half of spinach mixture. Arrange half of ravioli in a single layer over spinach mixture. Repeat layers once. Top with remaining sausage mixture.
4. Bake at 375° for 30 minutes. Sprinkle with shredded cheese, and bake 5 to 8 minutes or until hot and bubbly.

Note: We tested with Buitoni Pesto with Basil.

Rosemary Grilled Chicken Thighs with Sautéed Garlic Spinach and Two-Cheese Grits

MAKES: 4 to 6 servings ❋ **HANDS-ON TIME:** 10 min.
TOTAL TIME: 1 hr., 48 min., including spinach and grits

1	garlic clove, pressed	½	tsp. pepper
1	Tbsp. olive oil	1½	lb. skinned and boned chicken thighs**
2	Tbsp. Dijon mustard	½	lemon
2	Tbsp. honey		Sautéed Garlic Spinach
1	tsp. salt		Two-Cheese Grits
1	tsp. chopped fresh rosemary*		

1. Combine garlic and next 6 ingredients in a large heavy-duty zip-top plastic bag, squeezing bag to combine ingredients. Add chicken, turning to coat, and seal bag. Chill 1 to 24 hours.
2. Preheat grill to 350° to 400° (medium-high) heat. Remove chicken from marinade, discarding marinade. Grill chicken, covered with grill lid, 5 to 7 minutes on each side. Transfer chicken to a large piece of aluminum foil. Squeeze juice from lemon over chicken; fold foil around chicken, covering chicken completely. Let stand 10 minutes. Serve over Sautéed Garlic Spinach and Two-Cheese Grits.

*Fresh thyme, cilantro, or oregano may be substituted.
**1½ lb. skinned and boned chicken breasts may be substituted.

Sautéed Garlic Spinach

MAKES: 4 servings ❋ **HANDS-ON TIME:** 8 min. ❋ **TOTAL TIME:** 8 min.

1	garlic clove, pressed	1	(10-oz.) package fresh spinach
1	tsp. olive oil		Salt and pepper to taste

1. Sauté garlic in hot oil in a nonstick skillet over medium-high heat 30 seconds. Add spinach; cook 2 to 3 minutes or until spinach wilts. Sprinkle with salt and pepper to taste. Serve with slotted spoon or tongs.

Two-Cheese Grits

MAKES: 4 servings ❋ **HANDS-ON TIME:** 5 min. ❋ **TOTAL TIME:** 10 min.

1	tsp. salt	½	cup (2 oz.) shredded Parmesan cheese
1	cup uncooked quick-cooking grits	2	Tbsp. butter
1	cup (4 oz.) shredded Cheddar cheese		Pepper to taste

1. Bring 4 cups water and salt to a boil in a 3-qt. saucepan. Whisk in grits; reduce heat to medium-low, and cook 5 to 6 minutes or until tender. Remove from heat; stir in cheeses and butter. Sprinkle with pepper to taste.

Chicken Cutlets with Pecan Sauce

MAKES: 4 servings * **HANDS-ON TIME:** 23 min. * **TOTAL TIME:** 23 min.

½ cup pecans
¼ cup butter, divided
4 chicken cutlets (about 1¼ lb.)
1 tsp. salt
½ tsp. pepper
3 Tbsp. all-purpose flour

3 Tbsp. olive oil
½ cup chicken broth
1 Tbsp. brown sugar
2 Tbsp. cider vinegar
½ tsp. dried thyme

1. Heat pecans and 2 Tbsp. butter in a large nonstick skillet over medium-low heat, stirring often, 2 to 3 minutes or until toasted and fragrant. Remove from skillet.

2. Sprinkle chicken with salt and pepper. Dredge in flour.

3. Cook chicken in hot oil in skillet over medium heat 3 to 4 minutes on each side or until golden brown and done. Transfer to a serving platter. Top with pecans.

4. Add chicken broth to skillet, and cook 2 minutes, stirring to loosen particles from bottom of skillet. Add brown sugar, vinegar, and thyme, and cook 3 to 4 minutes or until sugar melts and sauce slightly thickens. Whisk in remaining 2 Tbsp. butter. Serve sauce over chicken.

Lemon Chicken

MAKES: 8 servings * **HANDS-ON TIME:** 30 min. * **TOTAL TIME:** 30 min.

4 skinned and boned chicken breasts
   (about 1½ lb.)
1 tsp. salt
½ tsp. pepper
⅓ cup all-purpose flour
4 Tbsp. butter, divided

2 Tbsp. olive oil, divided
¼ cup chicken broth
¼ cup lemon juice
8 lemon slices
¼ cup chopped fresh flat-leaf parsley

1. Cut each chicken breast in half lengthwise. Place chicken between 2 sheets of heavy-duty plastic wrap; flatten to ¼-inch thickness, using a rolling pin or flat side of a meat mallet. Sprinkle chicken with salt and pepper. Lightly dredge chicken in flour, shaking off excess.

2. Melt 1 Tbsp. butter with 1 Tbsp. olive oil in a large nonstick skillet over medium-high heat. Cook half of chicken in skillet 2 to 3 minutes on each side or until golden brown and done. Transfer chicken to a serving platter, and keep warm. Repeat procedure with 1 Tbsp. butter and remaining olive oil and chicken.

3. Add broth and lemon juice to skillet; cook 1 to 2 minutes or until sauce is slightly thickened, stirring to loosen particles from bottom of skillet. Add lemon slices.

4. Remove skillet from heat. Add parsley and remaining 2 Tbsp. butter; stir until butter melts. Pour sauce over chicken. Serve immediately.

Chicken Cutlets
with Pecan Sauce

Creamy Slow-Cooker Chicken

MAKES: 6 servings ✳ **HANDS-ON TIME:** 20 min. ✳ **TOTAL TIME:** 4 hr., 20 min.

This versatile low-fat recipe can be used in lots of innovative ways. Shred the cooked chicken, and toss with hot cooked pasta. Create a casserole, or jump-start a filling for easy enchiladas or a fast pot pie. Or serve with roasted vegetables and rice.

6	skinned and boned chicken breasts (about 2½ lb.)
2	tsp. seasoned salt
2	Tbsp. canola oil
1	(10¾-oz.) can reduced-fat cream of mushroom soup
1	(8-oz.) package ⅓-less-fat cream cheese
½	cup dry white wine
1	(0.7-oz.) envelope Italian dressing mix
1	(8-oz.) package sliced fresh mushrooms

1. Sprinkle chicken with seasoned salt. Cook chicken, in batches, in hot oil in a large skillet over medium-high heat 2 to 3 minutes on each side or just until browned. Transfer chicken to a 5-qt. slow cooker, reserving drippings in skillet.

2. Add soup and next 3 ingredients to hot drippings in skillet. Cook over medium heat, stirring constantly, 2 to 3 minutes or until cream cheese melts and mixture is smooth.

3. Arrange mushrooms over chicken in slow cooker. Spoon soup mixture over mushrooms. Cover and cook on LOW 4 hours. Stir well before serving.

Note: We tested with Good Seasons Italian All Natural Salad Dressing & Recipe Mix.

Note: To make ahead, prepare recipe as directed. Transfer to a 13- x 9-inch baking dish, and cool completely. Freeze up to 1 month. Thaw in refrigerator 8 to 24 hours. To reheat, cover tightly with aluminum foil, and bake at 325° for 45 minutes. Uncover and bake 15 minutes or until thoroughly heated.

Stove-top Chicken Pot Pie

MAKES: 6 to 8 servings ❋ **HANDS-ON TIME:** 35 min. ❋ **TOTAL TIME:** 35 min.

A family-size rotisserie chicken yields the perfect amount of chopped cooked chicken for this recipe.

8	frozen buttermilk biscuits	1	cup low-sodium fat-free chicken broth
1	small sweet onion, diced	½	cup dry white wine
1	Tbsp. canola oil	½	(8-oz.) package ⅓-less-fat cream cheese,
1	(8-oz.) package sliced fresh mushrooms		cubed
4	cups chopped cooked chicken	½	(0.7-oz.) envelope Italian dressing mix
1	(10¾-oz.) can reduced-fat cream of		(about 2 tsp.)
	mushroom soup	1	cup frozen baby peas, thawed

1. Bake biscuits according to package directions.

2. Meanwhile, sauté onion in hot oil in a large skillet over medium-high heat 5 minutes or until golden. Add mushrooms, and sauté 5 minutes or until tender. Stir in chicken and next 5 ingredients; cook, stirring frequently, 5 minutes or until cheese melts and mixture is thoroughly heated. Stir in peas, and cook 2 minutes. Spoon chicken mixture over hot split biscuits.

test kitchen tip: how to select sauté equipment

■ Use either a skillet (a wide pan with sloped sides) or sauté pan (a wide pan with straight sides). Both have a large surface area, so food is less likely to become overcrowded. Choose a pan with a dense bottom that evenly distributes heat. Nonstick, anodized aluminum, and stainless steel options work well.

Southern-Style Chicken Pot Pie

MAKES: 6 to 8 servings ✳ **HANDS-ON TIME:** 31 min. ✳ **TOTAL TIME:** 1 hr., 41 min.

½   cup butter
2   medium leeks, sliced
½   cup all-purpose flour
1   (14-oz.) can chicken broth
3   cups chopped cooked chicken
1½   cups frozen cubed hash browns with onions and peppers

1   cup matchstick carrots
⅓   cup chopped fresh flat-leaf parsley
½   tsp. salt
½   tsp. freshly ground pepper
½   (14.1-oz.) package refrigerated piecrusts
1   large egg

1. Preheat oven to 375°. Melt butter in a large skillet over medium heat; add leeks, and sauté 3 minutes. Sprinkle with flour; cook, stirring constantly, 3 minutes. Whisk in chicken broth; bring to a boil, whisking constantly. Remove from heat; stir in chicken and next 5 ingredients.

2. Unfold piecrust on a lightly floured surface. Using width of a ruler as a guide, cut piecrust into 9 (1-inch-wide) strips. Arrange strips in a lattice design over filling. Whisk together egg and 1 Tbsp. water, and brush over top of pie.

3. Bake at 375° on lower oven rack 55 to 60 minutes or until browned. Let stand 15 minutes.

Come in from the cold, and rediscover an old-fashioned favorite chicken pot pie.

Chicken Tetrazzini

MAKES: 8 to 10 servings ❋ **HANDS-ON TIME:** 20 min. ❋ **TOTAL TIME:** 55 min.

1½ (8-oz.) packages vermicelli
½ cup butter
½ cup all-purpose flour
4 cups milk
½ cup dry white wine
2 Tbsp. chicken bouillon granules

1 tsp. seasoned pepper
2 cups freshly grated Parmesan cheese, divided
4 cups diced cooked chicken
1 (6-oz.) jar sliced mushrooms, drained
¾ cup slivered almonds

1. Preheat oven to 350°. Prepare pasta according to package directions.

2. Meanwhile, melt butter in a Dutch oven over low heat; whisk in flour until smooth. Cook, whisking constantly, 1 minute. Gradually whisk in milk and wine; cook over medium heat, whisking constantly, 8 to 10 minutes or until mixture is thickened and bubbly. Whisk in bouillon granules, seasoned pepper, and 1 cup Parmesan cheese.

3. Remove from heat; stir in chicken, mushrooms, and hot cooked pasta.

4. Spoon chicken mixture into a lightly greased 13- x 9-inch baking dish; sprinkle with slivered almonds and remaining 1 cup Parmesan cheese.

5. Bake at 350° for 35 minutes or until bubbly.

Oven Chicken
Risotto

Oven Chicken Risotto

MAKES: 6 servings ✻ **HANDS-ON TIME:** 20 min. ✻ **TOTAL TIME:** 1 hr.

Green beans complement this dish nicely.

2	Tbsp. butter
2½	cups chicken broth
1	cup uncooked Arborio rice (short-grain)
½	small onion, diced
½	tsp. salt

2	cups chopped deli-roasted chicken
1	(8-oz.) package fresh mozzarella cheese, cut into ½-inch cubes
1	cup cherry or grape tomatoes, halved
¼	cup shredded fresh basil

1. Preheat oven to 400°. Place butter in a 13- x 9-inch baking dish; bake 5 minutes or until melted. Stir in broth and next 3 ingredients.

2. Bake, covered, at 400° for 35 minutes. Remove from oven. Fluff rice with a fork. Stir in chicken, mozzarella, and tomatoes; sprinkle with basil. Serve immediately.

Easy Chicken and Dumplings

MAKES: 4 to 6 servings ✻ **HANDS-ON TIME:** 30 min. ✻ **TOTAL TIME:** 40 min.

Deli-roasted chicken, cream of chicken soup, and canned biscuits make a quick-and-tasty version of this favorite. One chicken yields about three cups of meat.

1	(32-oz.) container low-sodium fat-free chicken broth
3	cups shredded cooked chicken (about 1½ lb.)
1	(10¾-oz.) can reduced-fat cream of chicken soup

¼	tsp. poultry seasoning
1	(10-oz.) can refrigerated jumbo buttermilk biscuits
2	carrots, diced
3	celery ribs, diced

1. Bring first 4 ingredients to a boil in a Dutch oven over medium-high heat. Cover, reduce heat to low, and simmer, stirring occasionally, 5 minutes. Increase heat to medium-high; return to a low boil.

2. Place biscuits on a lightly floured surface. Roll or pat each biscuit to ⅛-inch thickness; cut into ½-inch-wide strips.

3. Drop strips, 1 at a time, into boiling broth mixture. Add carrots and celery. Cover, reduce heat to low, and simmer 15 to 20 minutes, stirring occasionally to prevent dumplings from sticking.

Lightened King Ranch Chicken Casserole

MAKES: 8 to 10 servings ✳ **HANDS-ON TIME:** 40 min. ✳ **TOTAL TIME:** 3 hr., 15 min.

1   (4½- to 5-lb.) whole chicken
2   celery ribs, cut into 3 pieces each
2   carrots, cut into 3 pieces each
2½ to 3 tsp. salt
1   Tbsp. butter
1   medium onion, chopped
1   medium-size green bell pepper, chopped
1   garlic clove, pressed
1   (10¾-oz.) can reduced-fat cream of mushroom soup

1   (10¾-oz.) can reduced-fat cream of chicken soup
2   (10-oz.) cans diced tomatoes and green chiles, drained
1   tsp. dried oregano
1   tsp. ground cumin
1   tsp. Mexican-style chili powder
3   cups grated 2% reduced-fat sharp Cheddar cheese
12 (6-inch) fajita-size corn tortillas, cut into ½-inch strips

1. If applicable, remove giblets from chicken, and reserve for another use. Rinse chicken.

2. Place chicken, celery, carrots, and salt in a large Dutch oven with water to cover. Bring to a boil over medium-high heat; reduce heat to low. Cover and simmer 50 minutes to 1 hour or until chicken is done. Remove from heat. Remove chicken from broth; cool 30 minutes. Remove and reserve ¾ cup cooking liquid. Strain any remaining liquid; reserve for another use.

3. Preheat oven to 350°. Melt butter in a large skillet over medium-high heat. Add onion, and sauté 6 to 7 minutes or until tender. Add bell pepper and garlic, and sauté 3 to 4 minutes. Stir in reserved ¾ cup cooking liquid, cream of mushroom soup, and next 5 ingredients. Cook, stirring occasionally, 8 minutes.

4. Skin and bone chicken; shred meat into bite-size pieces. Layer half of chicken in a lightly greased 13- x 9-inch baking dish. Top with half of soup mixture and 1 cup Cheddar cheese. Cover with half of corn tortilla strips. Repeat layers once. Top with remaining 1 cup cheese.

5. Bake, covered, at 350° for 50 minutes; uncover and bake for 10 to 15 minutes or until bubbly. Let stand 10 minutes before serving.

*1 tsp. chili powder and ⅛ tsp. ground red pepper may be substituted for Mexican-style chili powder.

Greek-Style Meatloaf Sandwiches

MAKES: 8 servings ❋ **HANDS-ON TIME:** 30 min. ❋ **TOTAL TIME:** 1 hr., 40 min.

½   cup frozen diced onion, red and green bell pepper, and celery

1   tsp. olive oil

2   lb. ground chicken

½   cup fine, dry breadcrumbs

⅓   cup light mayonnaise

2   large eggs, lightly beaten

2   Tbsp. chopped fresh flat-leaf parsley

2   tsp. Greek seasoning

½   tsp. lemon zest

¼   tsp. salt

¼   tsp. freshly ground pepper

4   pita rounds, cut in half

Toppings: sliced cucumber, sliced tomatoes, crumbled feta cheese, plain yogurt, kalamata olives, lettuce leaves

1. Preheat oven to 350°. Sauté onion, red and green bell pepper, and celery in hot oil in a small skillet over medium-high heat 5 to 7 minutes or until vegetables are tender.

2. Stir together ground chicken, next 8 ingredients, and sautéed vegetables in a large bowl just until combined.

3. Place mixture in a lightly greased 9- x 5-inch baking dish. Bake at 350° for 1 hour to 1 hour and 10 minutes or until a meat thermometer registers 165°. Let stand 10 minutes before slicing. Serve meatloaf slices in pita rounds with desired toppings.

Note: We tested with Cavender's All Purpose Greek Seasoning.

Turkey Tostadas with Spicy Cranberry-Chipotle Sauce

MAKES: 8 servings ＊ **HANDS-ON TIME:** 23 min. ＊ **TOTAL TIME:** 45 min., including sauce

Poblano peppers are about 5-inch-long hot green peppers. Their heat level can pack a punch, so judge intensity by how pungent the pepper smells when slicing.

1	large onion, sliced		8	tostada shells
1	poblano pepper, seeded and sliced		1	cup refried black beans
1	large red bell pepper, sliced			Spicy Cranberry-Chipotle Sauce
2	Tbsp. olive oil		1	cup crumbled queso fresco (fresh Mexican cheese)
3	cups shredded roasted turkey			
2	garlic cloves, minced		½	cup loosely packed fresh cilantro leaves
	Salt to taste		8	lime wedges

1. Preheat oven to 400°. Sauté first 3 ingredients in hot oil in a large nonstick skillet over medium-high heat 6 to 8 minutes or until onion is golden. Stir in turkey and garlic; cook 2 to 3 minutes or until thoroughly heated. Season with salt to taste.

2. Bake tostada shells on a baking sheet at 400° for 3 minutes. Spread shells with refried beans; top with turkey mixture. Drizzle with a small amount of Spicy Cranberry-Chipotle Sauce. Sprinkle with queso fresco.

3. Bake at 400° for 10 to 12 minutes or until thoroughly heated. Serve with fresh cilantro, lime wedges, and remaining sauce.

Spicy Cranberry-Chipotle Sauce

MAKES: about 1⅓ cups ＊ **HANDS-ON TIME:** 5 min. ＊ **TOTAL TIME:** 7 min.

1	cup whole-berry cranberry sauce		1	tsp. chili powder
⅓	cup taco sauce		½	tsp. ground cumin
1	canned chipotle pepper in adobo sauce, minced			Salt to taste

1. Microwave first 5 ingredients at HIGH 2 to 3 minutes or until thickened, stirring halfway through. Season with salt to taste.

Harvest Pizza

Harvest Pizza

MAKES: 4 servings ✳ **HANDS-ON TIME:** 20 min. ✳ **TOTAL TIME:** 38 min.

1   lb. bakery pizza dough
Plain yellow or white cornmeal
1   cup mashed sweet potatoes or leftover sweet potato casserole (without toppings)
1   cup shredded roasted turkey

1   cup shredded spinach
½   cup sliced shiitake mushrooms
½   cup sliced red onion
1½   cups (6 oz.) shredded Havarti cheese
1   tsp. freshly ground Italian seasoning

1. Preheat oven to 450°. Roll pizza dough into a 12-inch circle. Transfer to a baking sheet sprinkled with cornmeal. Spread mashed sweet potatoes over dough. Top with turkey and remaining ingredients. Bake directly on oven rack at 450° 18 minutes or until edges are browned.

Sizzling Flounder

MAKES: 4 servings ✳ **HANDS-ON TIME:** 10 min. ✳ **TOTAL TIME:** 31 min.

¼   cup grated Parmesan cheese
1   tsp. paprika
4   (6-oz.) flounder fillets
¾   tsp. salt

¼   tsp. pepper
½   cup butter
2   Tbsp. fresh lemon juice

1. Place 1 oven rack 5 inches from heat; place a second rack in middle of oven. Combine Parmesan cheese and paprika. Season fish with salt and pepper.
2. Preheat oven to 450°. Heat butter in a broiler-safe 13- x 9-inch baking dish in oven 8 minutes or until butter melts and begins to brown. Place fish in hot butter, skin sides up.
3. Bake at 450° on middle oven rack 10 minutes. Carefully flip fish, and baste with pan juices. Sprinkle with lemon juice and Parmesan cheese mixture. Bake 5 more minutes or just until fish flakes with a fork. Remove from oven; increase oven temperature to broil.
4. Broil fish on oven rack 5 inches from heat 2 to 3 minutes or until bubbly and golden brown.

All the Trimmings

*Make these side dishes the star
of your holiday meal.*

Asparagus-New Potato Hash

Asparagus-New Potato Hash

MAKES: 8 servings ❋ **HANDS-ON TIME:** 40 min. ❋ **TOTAL TIME:** 1 hr.

1 lb. small red potatoes
1 lb. fresh asparagus
2 shallots, minced
2 Tbsp. olive oil
1 tsp. chopped fresh thyme
1 tsp. salt

½ tsp. pepper
2 tsp. fresh lemon juice
⅓ cup crumbled farmer's cheese or queso fresco (fresh Mexican cheese)

Garnish: lemon slices

1. Bring potatoes and salted water to cover to a boil in a Dutch oven over medium-high heat. Cook 15 minutes or just until tender; drain well. Cool 15 minutes; cut into quarters.

2. Snap off and discard tough ends of asparagus. Cut asparagus into ½-inch pieces.

3. Sauté shallots in hot oil in a large nonstick skillet 1 minute. Add asparagus, thyme, and next 3 ingredients; sauté 2 to 3 minutes or until asparagus is crisp-tender. Add potatoes, and sauté 3 minutes or until mixture is thoroughly heated. Remove from heat, and sprinkle with cheese. Garnish, if desired.

Note: We tested with Chapel Hill Creamery farmer's cheese.

Roasted Orange-Ginger Asparagus

MAKES: 6 to 8 servings ❋ **HANDS-ON TIME:** 15 min. ❋ **TOTAL TIME:** 30 min.

2 lb. fresh asparagus
¼ cup orange juice
2 Tbsp. olive oil
1 Tbsp. grated fresh ginger

1 Tbsp. Dijon mustard
½ tsp. salt
¼ tsp. pepper

1. Preheat oven to 400°. Snap off and discard tough ends of asparagus; place asparagus on a lightly greased baking sheet. Whisk together orange juice, olive oil, and next 4 ingredients; drizzle mixture over asparagus, tossing to coat.

2. Bake at 400° for 15 minutes or to desired degree of tenderness, turning once after 8 minutes.

Bacon-Brown Sugar Brussels Sprouts

MAKES: 6 to 8 servings ❋ **HANDS-ON TIME:** 20 min. ❋ **TOTAL TIME:** 31 min.

4   bacon slices
1   (14-oz.) can chicken broth
1   Tbsp. brown sugar

1   tsp. salt
1½ lb. Brussels sprouts, trimmed and halved

1. Cook bacon in a Dutch oven over medium heat 10 minutes or until crisp. Remove bacon, and drain on paper towels, reserving drippings in Dutch oven. Crumble bacon.

2. Add broth, brown sugar, and salt to drippings in Dutch oven; bring to a boil. Stir in Brussels sprouts. Cover and cook 6 to 8 minutes or until tender. Transfer Brussels sprouts to a serving bowl using a slotted spoon, and sprinkle with bacon. Serve immediately.

Sprouts and Cauliflower

MAKES: 6 servings ❋ **HANDS-ON TIME:** 16 min. ❋ **TOTAL TIME:** 26 min.

2   Tbsp. butter
1   garlic clove, pressed
¼   cup Italian-seasoned breadcrumbs
½   tsp. salt, divided
2¼ cups trimmed Brussels sprouts (about 1 lb.), halved

2   (10-oz.) packages fresh cauliflower florets (about 3 cups)
1   tsp. fresh lemon juice
¼   tsp. freshly ground pepper

1. Melt butter in a small skillet over medium heat; add garlic, and sauté 1 minute. Stir in breadcrumbs and ¼ tsp. salt, and cook, stirring occasionally, 3 to 4 minutes or until lightly toasted. Remove from heat.

2. Arrange Brussels sprouts in a steamer basket over boiling water. Cover and steam 8 minutes or until crisp-tender. Add cauliflower. Cover and steam 2 to 3½ minutes or just until tender. Transfer Brussels sprouts and cauliflower to a serving dish; sprinkle with lemon juice, pepper, and remaining ¼ tsp. salt, and toss to combine. Sprinkle with breadcrumb mixture; serve immediately.

Bacon-Brown Sugar
Brussels Sprouts

Home-Style
Butter Beans

Home-Style Butter Beans

MAKES: 6 to 8 servings ✻ **HANDS-ON TIME:** 16 min. ✻ **TOTAL TIME:** 2 hr., 21 min.

Try substituting frozen baby lima beans for the frozen butter beans.

5	bacon slices, diced	¼	cup butter
1	small onion, minced	2	tsp. salt
½	cup firmly packed brown sugar	1	tsp. cracked pepper
1	(16-oz.) package frozen butter beans		

1. Cook bacon and onion in a large Dutch oven over medium heat 5 to 7 minutes. Add brown sugar, and cook, stirring occasionally, 1 to 2 minutes or until sugar dissolves. Stir in butter beans and butter until butter melts and beans are thoroughly coated. Stir in 12 cups water.

2. Bring to a boil over medium-high heat; reduce heat to low, and simmer, stirring occasionally, 2 hours or until beans are very tender and liquid is thickened and just below top of beans. Stir in salt and pepper.

Sweet-and-Sour Green Beans

MAKES: 8 to 10 servings ✻ **HANDS-ON TIME:** 27 min. ✻ **TOTAL TIME:** 27 min.

6	bacon slices, cut into 1-inch pieces	2	Tbsp. cider vinegar
½	medium onion, chopped	2	Tbsp. sugar
2	(16-oz.) packages frozen whole or cut green beans		Salt and pepper to taste

1. Cook bacon and onion in a Dutch oven over medium heat, stirring often, 6 to 8 minutes or until browned. Transfer bacon mixture to a plate, reserving drippings in Dutch oven.

2. Cook beans in hot drippings, stirring often, 8 to 10 minutes or to desired degree of tenderness. Stir in vinegar, sugar, and bacon mixture. Cook, stirring often, 3 minutes or until thoroughly heated. Season with salt and pepper to taste.

Green Beans with Goat Cheese, Tomatoes, and Almonds

MAKES: 6 to 8 servings ✻ **HANDS-ON TIME:** 21 min. ✻ **TOTAL TIME:** 27 min.

½ cup sliced almonds
2 lb. haricots verts (tiny green beans), trimmed
3 Tbsp. sherry vinegar*
2 Tbsp. fresh lemon juice
¾ tsp. salt

½ tsp. pepper
⅓ cup olive oil
1 pt. cherry tomatoes, halved
2 shallots, thinly sliced
2 garlic cloves, minced
½ (4-oz.) goat cheese log, crumbled

1. Preheat oven to 350°. Bake almonds in a single layer in a shallow pan 6 to 8 minutes or until lightly toasted and fragrant, stirring halfway through.

2. Cook green beans in boiling salted water to cover 6 to 8 minutes or until crisp-tender; drain. Plunge beans into ice water to stop the cooking process; drain.

3. Whisk together vinegar and next 3 ingredients in a large bowl; add olive oil in a slow, steady stream, whisking constantly until blended and smooth. Add cherry tomatoes, shallots, garlic, and green beans; toss to coat.

4. Top green bean mixture with crumbled goat cheese and toasted almonds.

*White wine vinegar may be substituted.

Southern-Style Collard Greens

Southern-Style Collard Greens

MAKES: 10 to 12 servings ❋ **HANDS-ON TIME:** 1 hr., 4 min. ❋ **TOTAL TIME:** 3 hr., 4 min.

12 hickory-smoked bacon slices, finely chopped

2 medium-size sweet onions, finely chopped

¾ lb. smoked ham, chopped

6 garlic cloves, finely chopped

3 (32-oz.) containers chicken broth

3 (1-lb.) packages fresh collard greens, washed and trimmed

⅓ cup apple cider vinegar

1 Tbsp. sugar

1 tsp. salt

¾ tsp. pepper

1. Cook bacon in a 10-qt. stockpot over medium heat 10 to 12 minutes or until almost crisp. Add onion, and sauté 8 minutes; add ham and garlic, and sauté 1 minute. Stir in remaining ingredients. Cook 2 hours or to desired degree of tenderness.

Grilled Ratatouille

MAKES: 4 servings ❋ **HANDS-ON TIME:** 33 min. ❋ **TOTAL TIME:** 1 hr., 3 min.

1 medium zucchini

1 small eggplant

2 tsp. salt, divided

2 Tbsp. olive oil

2 garlic cloves, chopped

1 tsp. chopped fresh thyme leaves

¼ tsp. pepper

1 red or green bell pepper, cut into 1-inch pieces

1 medium onion, coarsely chopped

1 cup grape tomatoes, halved

1. Cut zucchini in half lengthwise; cut lengthwise into ¼-inch-thick slices. Peel eggplant, and cut into 1-inch cubes. Sprinkle eggplant with 1 tsp. salt, and let stand 30 minutes.
2. Meanwhile, stir together olive oil, next 3 ingredients, and remaining 1 tsp. salt. Let stand 20 minutes. Rinse eggplant, and pat dry.
3. Preheat grill to 300° to 350° (medium) heat. Combine eggplant, zucchini, bell pepper, onion, and olive oil mixture in a large bowl, tossing to combine. Grill vegetable mixture in a lightly greased grill wok or metal basket, stirring occasionally, 15 minutes. Stir in tomatoes, and grill 3 more minutes or until tomatoes are tender.

Carrot Orzo

MAKES: 6 to 8 servings ✳ **HANDS-ON TIME:** 41 min. ✳ **TOTAL TIME:** 41 min.

Though made with orzo rather than rice, this colorful dish is similar to risotto.

8 oz. carrots, cut into 1-inch pieces (about 2 cups)	1 tsp. salt
2½ cups chicken broth	½ tsp. pepper
3 Tbsp. butter	1 cup freshly grated Parmesan cheese
1 medium onion, chopped	3 Tbsp. chopped fresh chives
2 cups uncooked orzo pasta	1 tsp. chopped fresh thyme
2 garlic cloves, minced	Garnish: Carrot curls

1. Process carrots in a food processor 15 seconds or until finely chopped.

2. Combine 2½ cups water and broth in a microwave-safe measuring cup. Microwave at HIGH 5 minutes or until very hot.

3. Meanwhile, melt butter in a large saucepan over medium heat. Add carrots and onion, and cook, stirring occasionally, 5 minutes or until tender. Add orzo and garlic, and cook 1 minute.

4. Slowly stir hot broth mixture, salt, and pepper into orzo mixture. Cook, stirring often, 15 minutes or until liquid is absorbed.

5. Stir in cheese, chives, and thyme until blended. Serve orzo immediately. Garnish, if desired.

Honey-Glazed Carrots

MAKES: 6 servings ✳ **HANDS-ON TIME:** 13 min. ✳ **TOTAL TIME:** 28 min.

1 (1-lb.) package whole carrots, diagonally sliced	½ tsp. orange zest
2 Tbsp. butter	½ tsp. salt
2 Tbsp. honey	¼ tsp. freshly ground pepper
	1 Tbsp. chopped fresh parsley

1. Bring 1½ qt. water to a boil in a Dutch oven over medium heat. Add carrots; cook 10 minutes or until tender. Drain well. Return carrots to Dutch oven; add butter and next 4 ingredients. Cook, stirring occasionally, 3 to 5 minutes or until glazed. Stir in parsley. Serve immediately.

Carrot Orzo

Browned Butter Cauliflower Mash

Browned Butter Cauliflower Mash

MAKES: about 6 servings ❋ **HANDS-ON TIME:** 15 min. ❋ **TOTAL TIME:** 15 min.

1 head medium cauliflower (about 2 lb.), chopped*	¼ cup grated Parmesan cheese
½ cup sour cream	1 Tbsp. chopped fresh chives
¾ tsp. salt	2 Tbsp. butter
½ tsp. pepper	Garnish: fresh chives

1. Fill a large Dutch oven with water to depth of ¼ inch. Arrange cauliflower in Dutch oven. Cook, covered, over medium-high heat 7 to 10 minutes or until tender. Drain.

2. Process cauliflower, sour cream, salt, and pepper in a food processor 30 seconds to 1 minute or until smooth, stopping to scrape down sides as needed. Stir in Parmesan cheese and chives. Place in a bowl.

3. If desired, microwave mixture at HIGH 1 to 2 minutes or until thoroughly heated, stirring at 1-minute intervals.

4. Cook butter in a small heavy saucepan over medium heat, stirring constantly, 4 to 5 minutes or until butter begins to turn golden brown. Remove from heat, and immediately drizzle butter over cauliflower mixture. Garnish, if desired. Serve immediately.

*2 (16-oz.) bags frozen cauliflower may be substituted. Cook cauliflower according to package directions. Proceed with recipe as directed, beginning with Step 2.

Roasted Carrots

MAKES: 6 to 8 servings ❋ **HANDS-ON TIME:** 10 min. ❋ **TOTAL TIME:** 45 min.

You can use bagged baby carrots, but young carrots with tops taste better (pictured on page 89).

3 lb. small carrots with tops	¾ tsp. salt
1 Tbsp. olive oil	¼ tsp. pepper

1. Preheat oven to 450°. Peel carrots, if desired. Trim tops to 1 inch.

2. Toss carrots with oil, salt, and pepper. Place on a 17- x 12-inch jelly-roll pan.

3. Bake at 450° for 20 minutes, stirring once. Reduce heat to 325°, and bake, stirring occasionally, 15 minutes or until carrots are browned and tender.

Classic Parmesan Scalloped Potatoes

MAKES: 8 to 10 servings * **HANDS-ON TIME:** 20 min. * **TOTAL TIME:** 1 hr., 15 min.

Gently stirring twice while baking promotes even cooking and creaminess to this dish. Pull out of the oven, stir once more, then sprinkle with cheese, and continue baking without stirring for a casserole that's golden brown on top.

2	lb. Yukon gold potatoes, peeled and thinly sliced	2	garlic cloves, chopped
3	cups whipping cream	1½	tsp. salt
¼	cup chopped fresh flat-leaf parsley	¼	tsp. freshly ground pepper
		½	cup grated Parmesan cheese

1. Preheat oven to 400°. Layer potatoes in a 13- x 9-inch or 3-qt. baking dish.

2. Stir together cream and next 4 ingredients in a large bowl. Pour cream mixture over potatoes.

3. Bake at 400° for 30 minutes, stirring gently every 10 minutes. Sprinkle with cheese; bake 15 to 20 minutes or until bubbly and golden brown. Let stand on a wire rack 10 minutes before serving.

TRY THIS TWIST!

Gruyère Scalloped Potatoes: Substitute finely shredded Gruyère cheese for Parmesan. Reduce parsley to 2 Tbsp. and salt to 1 tsp. Prepare recipe as directed, stirring 1 tsp. freshly ground Italian seasoning into cream mixture in Step 2.

Note: We tested with McCormick Italian Herb Seasoning Grinder.

Bacon-and-Blue Cheese Mashed Potato Bake

MAKES: 6 to 8 servings * **HANDS-ON TIME:** 25 min. * **TOTAL TIME:** 50 min.

4	lb. baking potatoes	½	tsp. pepper
2	tsp. salt	1	tsp. salt
1¼	cups warm buttermilk	1	(4-oz.) wedge blue cheese, crumbled
½	cup warm milk	8	cooked and crumbled bacon slices
¼	cup melted butter		

1. Preheat oven to 350°. Peel potatoes; cut into 2-inch pieces. Bring potatoes, 2 tsp. salt, and water to cover to a boil in a large Dutch oven over medium-high heat; boil 20 minutes or until tender. Drain. Return potatoes to Dutch oven, reduce heat to low, and cook, stirring occasionally, 3 to 5 minutes or until potatoes are dry.

2. Mash potatoes with a potato masher to desired consistency. Stir in warm buttermilk, warm milk, melted butter, pepper, and 1 tsp. salt, stirring just until blended.

3. Stir in blue cheese and bacon, and spoon the mixture into a lightly greased 2½-qt. baking dish or 8 (10-oz.) ramekins. Bake at 350° for 35 minutes.

Classic Parmesan
Scalloped Potatoes

Browned Butter Mashed Potatoes

MAKES: 6 to 8 servings ⁕ **HANDS-ON TIME:** 24 min. ⁕ **TOTAL TIME:** 49 min.

¾ cup butter
4 lb. Yukon gold potatoes, peeled and cut
   into 2-inch pieces
1 Tbsp. salt, divided
¾ cup buttermilk

½ cup milk
¼ tsp. pepper
Garnishes: fresh parsley, rosemary, and
   thyme sprigs

1. Cook butter in a 2-qt. heavy saucepan over medium heat, stirring constantly, 6 to 8 minutes or just until butter begins to turn golden brown. Immediately remove pan from heat, and pour butter into a small bowl. (Butter will continue to darken if left in saucepan.) Reserve 1 to 2 Tbsp. browned butter.

2. Bring potatoes, 2 tsp. salt, and water to cover to a boil in a large Dutch oven over medium-high heat; boil 20 minutes or until tender. Drain; return potatoes to Dutch oven. Reduce heat to low, and cook, stirring occasionally, 3 to 5 minutes or until potatoes are dry.

3. Mash potatoes with a potato masher to desired consistency. Stir in browned butter, buttermilk, milk, pepper, and remaining 1 tsp. salt, stirring just until blended.

4. Transfer to a serving dish. Drizzle with reserved 1 to 2 Tbsp. browned butter. Garnish, if desired.

Note: To make ahead, prepare recipe as directed through Step 3. Place in a lightly greased 2½-qt. ovenproof serving dish; cover and chill up to 2 days. Let stand at room temperature 30 minutes. Bake, uncovered, at 350° for 35 to 40 minutes or until thoroughly heated. Drizzle with reserved browned butter, and garnish, if desired.

Browned butter mixed into the potatoes, as well as drizzled on top, adds to the intense flavor of this side.

Pecan-Ginger-Sweet Potato Cups

MAKES: 8 servings ✻ **HANDS-ON TIME:** 30 min. ✻ **TOTAL TIME:** 2 hr., 10 min.

6   small sweet potatoes (about 2¾ lb.)
4   large navel oranges
1   (14-oz.) can sweetened condensed milk
3   Tbsp. melted butter
2   tsp. vanilla extract
2   tsp. orange zest
¾   tsp. ground ginger
¼   tsp. salt

⅛   tsp. ground nutmeg
⅛   tsp. ground allspice
⅛   tsp. ground cinnamon
½   cup chopped pecans
1   cup miniature marshmallows
Garnishes: fresh rosemary sprigs, fresh
    cranberries

1. Preheat oven to 425°. Place sweet potatoes on an aluminum foil-lined baking sheet. Bake 45 minutes or until tender. Let stand 20 minutes. Reduce oven temperature to 350°.

2. Meanwhile, cut oranges in half crosswise. Scoop out pulp using a spoon, leaving peel intact. Reserve orange pulp for another use.

3. Peel sweet potatoes, and place potato pulp in a large bowl. Add condensed milk and next 8 ingredients. Beat at medium speed with an electric mixer until smooth, stopping occasionally to remove any tough fibers, if necessary. Spoon about ½ cup mixture into each orange cup. Place orange cups in a 13- x 9-inch baking dish.

4. Bake at 350° for 20 minutes. Remove from oven; top with pecans and marshmallows, pressing lightly to adhere. Bake 15 to 20 minutes or until marshmallows are melted and golden brown. Garnish, if desired.

Note: Scoop out orange cups and bake sweet potatoes up to 1 day ahead. Chill in separate zip-top plastic bags.

Lightened Squash Casserole

MAKES: 10 to 12 servings ❈ **HANDS-ON TIME:** 25 min. ❈ **TOTAL TIME:** 1 hr., 10 min.

3   lb. yellow squash
½   cup chopped sweet onion
1½ tsp. salt, divided
1   cup grated carrots
1   (10¾-oz.) can reduced-fat cream of chicken soup

1   (8-oz.) container light sour cream
¼   cup chopped fresh chives
½   cup crushed cornflakes cereal
½   cup crushed French fried onions
2   Tbsp. melted butter
¼   tsp. freshly ground pepper

1. Preheat oven to 350°. Cut squash into ¼-inch-thick slices; place in a Dutch oven. Add onion, 1 tsp. salt, and water to cover. Bring to a boil over medium-high heat, and cook 5 minutes; drain well, and pat squash dry with paper towels.

2. Stir together grated carrots, next 3 ingredients, and remaining ½ tsp. salt in a large bowl; fold in squash mixture. Spoon into a lightly greased 2-qt. oval baking dish.

3. Stir together cornflakes and next 3 ingredients in a small bowl. Sprinkle over squash mixture.

4. Bake at 350° for 30 to 35 minutes or until bubbly and golden brown, shielding with aluminum foil after 20 to 25 minutes to prevent excessive browning, if necessary. Let stand 10 minutes before serving.

Roasted Vegetables

MAKES: 8 servings ＊ **HANDS-ON TIME:** 30 min. ＊ **TOTAL TIME:** 1 hr., 30 min.

1	medium eggplant, peeled and cubed	1	red bell pepper, cut into 1-inch pieces
¼	tsp. salt	¼	cup olive oil
2	zucchini, sliced	1	Tbsp. chopped fresh rosemary
1	large sweet potato, peeled and sliced	¼	tsp. pepper
1	onion, peeled and cut into eighths		

1. Sprinkle eggplant with salt, and let stand 30 minutes. Pat dry.

2. Preheat oven to 400°. Toss together eggplant and remaining ingredients, and arrange in a single layer in 2 aluminum foil-lined jelly-roll pans.

3. Bake at 400° for 30 minutes or until vegetables are tender and golden brown. Season with salt to taste.

test kitchen tip: how to cube eggplant

■ Fresh eggplant has a sparkling jewel-like color with shiny, smooth skin. It should feel heavy in your hand and be firm but slightly springy. Use a vegetable peeler to peel off the skin and then cut into slices. Cut the slices into cubes.

Shrimp and
Grits Dressing

Shrimp and Grits Dressing

MAKES: 6 to 8 servings ✳ **HANDS-ON TIME:** 35 min. ✳ **TOTAL TIME:** 1 hr., 50 min.

1	lb. peeled, medium-size raw shrimp (51/60 count)	½	cup butter
3	cups chicken broth	3	large eggs, lightly beaten
½	tsp. salt	1	red bell pepper, diced
¼	tsp. ground red pepper	1	cup fine, dry breadcrumbs
1	cup uncooked regular grits	1	cup chopped green onions
		½	cup grated Parmesan cheese

1. Preheat oven to 325°. Devein shrimp, if desired.

2. Bring broth and next 2 ingredients to a boil in a large saucepan over medium-high heat. Whisk in grits, and return to a boil; reduce heat to low, and stir in butter. Cover and simmer, stirring occasionally, 10 minutes or until liquid is absorbed. Remove from heat.

3. Stir together eggs and next 4 ingredients in a large bowl. Gradually stir about one-fourth of hot grits mixture into egg mixture; add egg mixture to remaining hot grits mixture, stirring constantly. Stir in shrimp until blended. Pour grits mixture into a lightly greased 11- x 7-inch baking dish.

4. Bake at 325° for 55 minutes to 1 hour or until mixture is set. Let stand 10 minutes.

Cornbread Dressing

MAKES: 8 servings ✳ **HANDS-ON TIME:** 26 min. ✳ **TOTAL TIME:** 2 hr., 6 min.

½	cup butter, divided	1	small sweet onion, diced
1½	cups self-rising white buttermilk cornmeal mix	2	celery ribs, diced
½	cup all-purpose flour	2	Tbsp. finely chopped fresh sage
5	large eggs, divided	2	Tbsp. finely chopped fresh parsley
1½	cups buttermilk	2	tsp. seasoned pepper
1½	cups soft, fresh breadcrumbs	¼	tsp. salt
		2	(14-oz.) cans chicken broth

1. Preheat oven to 425°. Place ¼ cup butter in an 8-inch cast-iron skillet; heat in oven 4 minutes.

2. Stir together cornmeal mix and flour; whisk in 1 egg and buttermilk.

3. Pour hot butter from skillet into batter, and stir until blended. Pour batter into hot skillet.

4. Bake at 425° for 30 minutes or until golden brown. Reduce oven temperature to 400°. Remove cornbread from pan, and cool 20 minutes. Crumble cornbread into a large bowl; stir in soft, fresh breadcrumbs.

5. Melt remaining ¼ cup butter in skillet over medium heat; add diced onion and celery, and sauté 5 minutes. Stir in chopped sage and next 3 ingredients; sauté 1 minute. Remove from heat, and stir into cornbread mixture.

6. Whisk together chicken broth and remaining 4 eggs; stir into cornbread mixture. Pour into a lightly greased 9-inch square pan.

7. Bake at 400° for 50 to 55 minutes or until golden brown.

Note: We tested with White Lily Self-Rising Buttermilk Cornmeal Mix.

Roasted Vegetable Gnocchi with Spinach-Herb Pesto

MAKES: 4 servings ✳ **HANDS-ON TIME:** 10 min. ✳ **TOTAL TIME:** 55 min., including pesto

Dumpling-like gnocchi [NYOH-kee] are sold near the dried pastas.

6	yellow squash (about 1¼ lb.)	1	(16-oz.) package gnocchi*
8	sweet mini bell peppers		Spinach-Herb Pesto
2	Tbsp. olive oil	½	(5-oz.) package baby spinach
1	tsp. salt	¼	to ⅓ cup (1 to 1½ oz.) freshly grated
½	tsp. coarsely ground pepper		Parmesan cheese

1. Preheat oven to 425°. Cut squash into 1-inch pieces. Cut bell peppers in half lengthwise; remove seeds. Stir together squash, bell peppers, oil, salt, and ground pepper. Arrange vegetables in a single layer on a jelly-roll pan, and bake 15 minutes. Stir and bake 5 minutes or until tender and golden.

2. Cook gnocchi according to package directions in a Dutch oven; drain. Return to Dutch oven. Add Spinach-Herb Pesto to gnocchi, and toss to coat. Add squash mixture and spinach, and gently toss to combine. Sprinkle with Parmesan cheese. Serve immediately.

*Medium-size pasta shells may be substituted.

Note: We tested with Gia Russa Gnocchi with Potato.

Spinach-Herb Pesto

MAKES: ¾ cup ✳ **HANDS-ON TIME:** 15 min. ✳ **TOTAL TIME:** 15 min.

½	(5-oz.) package baby spinach	1	garlic clove, minced
1	Tbsp. chopped fresh cilantro	¼	tsp. salt
1	Tbsp. chopped fresh basil	½	cup (2 oz.) freshly grated Parmesan
1	tsp. lemon zest		cheese
2	Tbsp. lemon juice	¼	cup olive oil
1	tsp. chopped fresh mint		

1. Pulse first 8 ingredients in a food processor 6 to 7 times or until finely chopped. Add Parmesan cheese and oil; process until smooth, stopping to scrape down sides as needed. Use immediately, or store in refrigerator up to 48 hours. If chilled, let stand at room temperature 30 minutes before using; stir until blended.

Roasted Asparagus Salad

MAKES: 8 servings ❋ **HANDS-ON TIME:** 20 min. ❋ **TOTAL TIME:** 43 min.

1½ lb. fresh asparagus	1 cup halved cherry tomatoes
½ cup olive oil, divided	(about ½ pt.)
1½ Tbsp. chopped fresh basil, divided	½ cup chopped red bell pepper
½ tsp. lemon pepper	¼ cup finely chopped red onion
½ tsp. salt, divided	1 head Bibb lettuce, torn into bite-size
¼ cup balsamic vinegar	pieces
1 garlic clove, minced	1 avocado, sliced

1. Preheat oven to 425°. Snap off and discard tough ends of asparagus; remove scales with a vegetable peeler, if desired.

2. Stir together 1 Tbsp. olive oil, 1½ tsp. chopped basil, lemon pepper, and ¼ tsp. salt in a large bowl.

3. Add asparagus to olive oil mixture, and toss gently to coat. Place asparagus on a lightly greased baking sheet.

4. Bake asparagus at 425° for 13 to 15 minutes or to desired degree of tenderness. Cool 10 minutes.

5. Whisk together balsamic vinegar, garlic, and remaining 7 Tbsp. olive oil, 1 Tbsp. basil, and ¼ tsp. salt.

6. Toss together tomatoes, bell pepper, onion, and 1 Tbsp. balsamic vinegar mixture.

7. Arrange lettuce on individual serving plates. Top with tomato mixture and asparagus. Add avocado just before serving. Drizzle with remaining balsamic vinegar mixture.

Note: To make ahead, toss together tomatoes, bell pepper, and onion without dressing. Store these ready-to-use ingredients in an airtight container in the refrigerator up to 5 hours. The dressing and asparagus can also be made up to 8 hours before serving.

Baby Blue Salad with Fresh Pears

MAKES: 8 servings ✳ **HANDS-ON TIME:** 25 min.
TOTAL TIME: 55 min., including pecans and vinaigrette

2 (5-oz.) packages gourmet mixed salad
  greens
2 large Bartlett pears, cut into thin slices
1 qt. strawberries, quartered

4 oz. blue cheese, crumbled
Sweet-and-Spicy Pecans
Balsamic Vinaigrette

1. Place greens on 8 individual serving plates. Top with pears and strawberries. Sprinkle with blue cheese and pecans. Serve with Balsamic Vinaigrette.

Sweet-and-Spicy Pecans

MAKES: 1 cup ✳ **HANDS-ON TIME:** 15 min. ✳ **TOTAL TIME:** 25 min.

¼ cup sugar
1 cup warm water
1 cup pecan halves

2 Tbsp. sugar
1 Tbsp. chili powder
⅛ tsp. ground red pepper

1. Preheat oven to 350°. Stir together ¼ cup sugar and warm water until sugar dissolves. Add pecans, and soak 10 minutes. Drain, discarding syrup.
2. Combine 2 Tbsp. sugar, chili powder, and red pepper. Add pecans, tossing to coat. Place pecans on a lightly greased baking sheet. Bake pecans at 350° for 10 minutes or until golden brown, stirring once after 5 minutes.

Balsamic Vinaigrette

MAKES: 1⅔ cups ✳ **HANDS-ON TIME:** 10 min. ✳ **TOTAL TIME:** 10 min.

½ cup balsamic vinegar
3 Tbsp. Dijon mustard
3 Tbsp. honey
2 garlic cloves, minced

2 small shallots, minced
¼ tsp. salt
¼ tsp. pepper
1 cup olive oil

1. Whisk together first 7 ingredients until blended. Gradually add olive oil in a slow, steady stream, whisking constantly until blended.

Waldorf Spinach
Salad

Waldorf Spinach Salad

MAKES: 6 servings ✳ HANDS-ON TIME: 25 min. ✳ TOTAL TIME: 25 min.

¼   cup honey
3   Tbsp. vegetable oil
2   Tbsp. cider vinegar
½   tsp. dry mustard
¼   tsp. ground cinnamon
1   garlic clove, pressed
⅛   tsp. salt

1   (10-oz.) package fresh spinach, torn
2   large Gala apples, thinly sliced
4   oz. extra-sharp white Cheddar cheese, shaved
1   cup thinly sliced celery
1   cup honey-roasted cashews
½   cup golden raisins

1. Whisk together first 7 ingredients in a large serving bowl until well blended. Add spinach and remaining ingredients, tossing gently to coat. Serve immediately.

Easy Spinach, Pear, and Goat Cheese Salad

MAKES: 6 to 8 servings ✳ HANDS-ON TIME: 15 min. ✳ TOTAL TIME: 23 min.

½   cup coarsely chopped pecans
3   large Anjou pears
¼   cup orange juice
1   (6-oz.) package fresh baby spinach, thoroughly washed

1   (4-oz.) package goat cheese, crumbled
¼   tsp. freshly ground pepper
½   cup bottled olive oil vinaigrette

1. Preheat oven to 350°. Place pecans in a single layer in a shallow pan, and bake 7 to 8 minutes or until toasted and fragrant, stirring occasionally.
2. Peel and thinly slice pears. Toss in orange juice; drain, discarding juice.
3. Place spinach on a serving platter or in a large bowl. Top with pear slices. Sprinkle with goat cheese, pecans, and pepper. Drizzle with vinaigrette.

Note: We tested with Newman's Own Olive Oil & Vinegar Dressing.

Bread Basket

Turn your kitchen into a holiday bakery with this melt-in-your mouth selection of breads, rolls, and more.

Pimiento Cheese Rolls

MAKES: 1 dozen ✻ **HANDS-ON TIME:** 15 min. ✻ **TOTAL TIME:** 1 hr., 25 min.

1 **(26.4-oz.) package frozen biscuits**
All-purpose flour

2 **cups pimiento cheese**

1. Preheat oven to 375°. Arrange frozen biscuits, with sides touching, in 3 rows of 4 biscuits on a lightly floured surface. Let stand 30 to 45 minutes or until biscuits are thawed but cool to the touch.

2. Sprinkle thawed biscuits lightly with flour. Press biscuit edges together, and pat to form a 12- x 10-inch rectangle of dough; spread evenly with pimiento cheese.

3. Roll up, starting at one long end; cut into 12 (about 1-inch-thick) slices. Place one slice into each cup of 1 lightly greased (12-cup) muffin pan.

4. Bake at 375° for 20 to 25 minutes or until golden brown. Cool slightly, and remove from pan.

TRY THESE TWISTS!

Ham-and-Swiss Rolls: Omit pimiento cheese. Stir together ¼ cup each of softened butter, spicy brown mustard, and finely chopped sweet onion. Spread butter mixture evenly over 12- x 10-inch rectangle of thawed dough; sprinkle evenly with 1 cup each of shredded Swiss cheese and chopped cooked ham. Proceed with recipe as directed.

Sausage-and-Cheddar Rolls: Omit pimiento cheese. Spread ¼ cup softened butter evenly over 12- x 10-inch rectangle of thawed dough; sprinkle evenly with 1 cup each of shredded Cheddar cheese and cooked, crumbled sausage. Proceed with recipe as directed.

Ham-and-Swiss Rolls

Quick
Buttermilk
Biscuits

Walnut-Honey
Butter

Blackberry
Butter

Lemon-Herb
Butter

Quick Buttermilk Biscuits

MAKES: about 3 dozen ✳ **HANDS-ON TIME:** 10 min. ✳ **TOTAL TIME:** 22 min.

1 cup shortening

4 cups self-rising soft-wheat flour

1¾ cups buttermilk

1. Preheat oven to 425°. Cut shortening into flour with a pastry blender until crumbly. Add buttermilk, stirring just until dry ingredients are moistened.

2. Turn dough out onto a lightly floured surface, and knead lightly 4 to 5 times. Pat or roll dough to ¾-inch thickness, cut with a 1½-inch round cutter, and place on 2 lightly greased baking sheets.

3. Bake at 425° for 12 to 14 minutes or until lightly browned.

Note: To freeze, place unbaked biscuits on pans in freezer for 30 minutes or until frozen. Transfer frozen biscuits to zip-top plastic freezer bags, and freeze up to 3 months. Bake frozen biscuits at 425° on lightly greased baking sheets 14 to 16 minutes or until lightly browned.

SERVE WITH

Lemon-Herb Butter: Stir together ½ cup softened butter, 2 tsp. lemon zest, 1 tsp. chopped fresh chives, 1 tsp. chopped fresh oregano, and 1 tsp. chopped fresh parsley. MAKES: about ½ cup; HANDS-ON TIME: 5 min.; TOTAL TIME: 5 min.

Blackberry Butter: Stir together ½ cup softened butter and 3 Tbsp. blackberry preserves. MAKES: about ¾ cup; HANDS-ON TIME: 5 min.; TOTAL TIME: 5 min.

Walnut-Honey Butter: Bake ¼ cup finely chopped walnuts at 350° in a single layer in a pan 5 to 7 minutes or until lightly toasted, stirring halfway through. Cool 15 minutes. Stir together ½ cup softened butter, 2 Tbsp. honey, and walnuts. MAKES: about ¾ cup; HANDS-ON TIME: 5 min.; TOTAL TIME: 25 min.

Blueberry Streusel Muffins

MAKES: 1½ dozen. ✳ **HANDS-ON TIME:** 15 min. ✳ **TOTAL TIME:** 50 min.

Stock up on blueberries when they're in season and freeze to enjoy all year long. If using frozen blueberries, rinse and drain thawed berries; pat dry with paper towels. This will prevent discoloration of the batter.

BATTER:
- ¼ cup butter, softened
- ⅓ cup sugar
- 1 large egg
- 2⅓ cups all-purpose flour
- 1 Tbsp. plus 1 tsp. baking powder
- ½ tsp. salt
- 1 cup milk
- 1 tsp. vanilla extract
- 1½ cups fresh blueberries

STREUSEL TOPPING:
- ½ cup sugar
- ⅓ cup all-purpose flour
- ½ tsp. ground cinnamon
- ¼ cup butter, softened

1. Preheat oven to 375°. Lightly grease muffin pans.

2. Prepare Batter: Beat butter at medium speed with an electric mixer until creamy; gradually add ⅓ cup sugar, beating until light and fluffy. Add egg, beating well.

3. Combine 2⅓ cups flour, 1 Tbsp. plus 1 tsp. baking powder, and ½ tsp. salt; gradually add to butter mixture alternately with milk, beginning and ending with flour mixture and beating well after each addition. Stir in vanilla, and fold in blueberries. Spoon batter into 2 greased (12-cup) muffin pans, filling two-thirds full.

4. Prepare Streusel Topping: Combine ½ cup sugar, ⅓ cup flour, and ½ tsp. cinnamon; cut in ¼ cup butter with a pastry blender until crumbly. Sprinkle on top of muffin batter.

5. Bake at 375° for 35 minutes or until golden brown. Remove from pans immediately.

Sticky Bun-Pumpkin Muffins

MAKES: about 2 dozen ❋ **HANDS-ON TIME:** 20 min. ❋ **TOTAL TIME:** 1 hr.

2	cups pecan halves and pieces		1	Tbsp. pumpkin pie spice
½	cup butter, melted		1	tsp. baking soda
½	cup firmly packed light brown sugar		1	tsp. salt
2	Tbsp. light corn syrup		1	(15-oz.) can pumpkin
3½	cups all-purpose flour		1	cup canola oil
3	cups granulated sugar		4	large eggs

1. Preheat oven to 350°. Bake pecans in a single layer in a shallow pan 8 to 10 minutes or until toasted and fragrant, stirring halfway through.

2. Stir together melted butter and next 2 ingredients. Spoon 1 rounded teaspoonful butter mixture into each cup of 2 lightly greased (12-cup) muffin pans, and top each with 1 rounded tablespoonful pecans.

3. Stir together flour and next 4 ingredients in a large bowl, and make a well in center of mixture. Whisk together pumpkin, next 2 ingredients, and ⅔ cup water; add to dry ingredients, stirring just until moistened.

4. Spoon batter into prepared muffin pans, filling three-fourths full. Place an aluminum foil-lined jelly-roll pan on lower oven rack to catch any overflow.

5. Bake at 350° on middle oven rack for 25 to 30 minutes or until a wooden pick inserted in center comes out clean. Invert pan immediately to remove muffins, and arrange muffins on a wire rack. Spoon any topping remaining in muffin cups over muffins. Cool 5 minutes.

TRY THIS TWIST!

Pecan-Pumpkin Bread: Omit butter, brown sugar, and corn syrup. Substitute 1½ cups chopped pecans for 2 cups pecan halves and pieces; toast as directed in Step 1. Omit Step 2. Prepare batter as directed in Step 3; stir in pecans. Spoon batter into 2 greased and floured 9- x 5-inch loaf pans. Bake at 350° for 1 hour to 1 hour and 10 minutes or until a long wooden pick inserted in center comes out clean. Cool in pans on a wire rack 10 minutes. Remove from pans to wire rack, and cool completely (about 1 hour). MAKES: 2 loaves; HANDS-ON TIME: 20 min.; TOTAL TIME: 2 hr., 40 min.

Caramel-Nut Pull-Apart Bread

MAKES: 12 servings ❊ **HANDS-ON TIME:** 10 min. ❊ **TOTAL TIME:** 40 min.

This warm, gooey bread is swimming in sweet caramel. To enjoy it at its best, serve immediately.

1	cup plus 2 Tbsp. firmly packed brown sugar	1	cup chopped walnuts
4	tsp. ground cinnamon	¾	cup butter, melted
		3	(10-oz.) cans refrigerated biscuits

1. Preheat oven to 350°. Combine brown sugar, cinnamon, and walnuts in a small bowl. Stir in butter. Spoon half of sugar mixture in bottom of a lightly greased Bundt pan.

2. Cut each biscuit in half. Place half of biscuit halves alternately over sugar mixture. Spoon remaining sugar mixture over biscuits in pan, and top with remaining biscuit halves.

3. Bake at 350° for 30 to 35 minutes or until browned. Invert bread onto a serving platter immediately, spooning any brown sugar sauce left in pan over bread.

Pecan-Pumpkin Bread with Orange Marmalade-Cream Cheese Spread

MAKES: 2 loaves ❋ **HANDS-ON TIME:** 20 min. ❋ **TOTAL TIME:** 1 hr., 35 min.

3	cups sugar		1	Tbsp. pumpkin pie spice
1	cup vegetable oil		1	tsp. baking soda
4	large eggs		1	tsp. salt
1	(15-oz.) can unsweetened pumpkin		1½	cups chopped pecans, toasted
3½	cups all-purpose flour			Orange Marmalade-Cream Cheese Spread

1. Preheat oven to 350°. Beat together first 8 ingredients at low speed with an electric mixer 3 minutes or until blended. Add ⅔ cup water, beating until blended. Stir in pecans. Pour batter into 2 greased and floured 9- x 5-inch loaf pans.

2. Bake at 350° for 1 hour and 15 minutes or until a long wooden pick inserted in center of bread comes out clean. Cool in pans on a wire rack 10 minutes; remove from pans, and cool completely on wire rack. Serve with Orange Marmalade-Cream Cheese Spread.

Orange Marmalade-Cream Cheese Spread

MAKES: about 1½ cups ❋ **HANDS-ON TIME:** 5 min. ❋ **TOTAL TIME:** 5 min.

1	(8-oz.) package cream cheese, softened		1	tsp. orange zest
½	cup orange marmalade			

1. Stir together all ingredients until blended.

Praline-Apple Bread

MAKES: 1 loaf ✳ **HANDS-ON TIME:** 26 min. ✳ **TOTAL TIME:** 2 hr., 41 min.

1½ cups chopped pecans, divided
1 (8-oz.) container sour cream
1 cup granulated sugar
2 large eggs
1 Tbsp. vanilla extract
2 cups all-purpose flour
2 tsp. baking powder

½ tsp. baking soda
½ tsp. salt
1½ cups finely chopped, peeled Granny Smith apples (about ¾ lb.)
½ cup butter
½ cup firmly packed light brown sugar

1. Preheat oven to 350°. Bake ½ cup pecans in a single layer in a shallow pan 6 to 8 minutes or until toasted and fragrant, stirring after 4 minutes.

2. Beat together sour cream and next 3 ingredients at low speed with an electric mixer 2 minutes or until blended.

3. Stir together flour and next 3 ingredients. Add to sour cream mixture, beating just until blended. Stir in chopped apple and ½ cup toasted pecans. Spoon batter into a greased and floured 9- x 5-inch loaf pan. Sprinkle with remaining 1 cup chopped pecans; lightly press pecans into batter.

4. Bake at 350° for 1 hour to 1 hour and 5 minutes or until a wooden pick inserted into center comes out clean, shielding with aluminum foil after 50 minutes to prevent excessive browning. Cool in pan on a wire rack 10 minutes; remove from pan to wire rack.

5. Bring butter and brown sugar to a boil in a 1-qt. heavy saucepan over medium heat, stirring constantly; boil 1 minute. Remove from heat, and spoon over top of bread; cool completely (about 1 hour).

Note: To freeze, cool bread completely; wrap in plastic wrap and then in aluminum foil. Freeze up to 3 months. Thaw at room temperature.

Butternut Squash Spoon Bread

MAKES: 8 servings ✳ **HANDS-ON TIME:** 25 min. ✳ **TOTAL TIME:** 1 hr., 10 min.

2   cups buttermilk
4   large eggs, separated
2   cups thawed, frozen unseasoned,
    puréed butternut squash
⅓   cup freshly grated Parmesan cheese
1   cup stone-ground white cornmeal

1   tsp. baking powder
1   tsp. chopped fresh rosemary
½   tsp. baking soda
½   tsp. salt
¼   cup butter, melted

1. Preheat oven to 350°. Cook buttermilk in a heavy saucepan over medium-high heat, stirring often, 4 to 6 minutes or until bubbles appear around edges (do not boil); remove from heat. (Mixture may curdle.)

2. Lightly beat egg yolks in a large bowl; stir in squash and cheese. Combine cornmeal and next 4 ingredients in a small bowl. Stir cornmeal mixture into squash mixture. Pour warm buttermilk over squash mixture; whisk until smooth. Let stand 15 minutes or until lukewarm.

3. Brush a 2½- to 3-qt. baking dish or 12-inch cast-iron skillet with 1 Tbsp. melted butter; stir remaining melted butter into squash mixture.

4. Beat egg whites at high speed with an electric mixer until stiff peaks form. Carefully fold into squash mixture. Pour mixture into prepared baking dish.

5. Bake at 350° for 30 to 35 minutes or until top is golden and a wooden pick inserted in center comes out clean.

Note: We tested with Bird's Eye Butternut Squash. Buy 2 (12-oz.) packages to measure 2 cups.

Sour Cream Cornbread

MAKES: 8 servings ✳ **HANDS-ON TIME:** 10 min. ✳ **TOTAL TIME:** 37 min.

1½ cups self-rising white cornmeal mix
½ cup all-purpose flour
1 (14.75-oz.) can low-sodium cream-style corn
1 (8-oz.) container light sour cream

3 large eggs, lightly beaten
2 Tbsp. chopped fresh cilantro
½ cup (2 oz.) 2% reduced-fat shredded Cheddar cheese (optional)

1. Preheat oven to 450°. Heat a 10-inch cast-iron skillet in oven 5 minutes.

2. Stir together cornmeal mix and flour in a large bowl; add corn and next 3 ingredients, stirring just until blended. Pour batter into hot lightly greased skillet. Top with cheese, if desired.

3. Bake at 450° for 22 to 24 minutes or until golden brown and cornbread pulls away from sides of skillet.

Buttermilk Cornbread

MAKES: 8 servings ✳ **HANDS-ON TIME:** 5 min. ✳ **TOTAL TIME:** 35 min.

1¼ cups all-purpose flour
1 cup plus 3 Tbsp. plain white cornmeal
¼ cup sugar
1 Tbsp. baking powder

1 tsp. salt
¼ cup butter, melted
2 large eggs
1 cup buttermilk

1. Preheat oven to 400°. Lightly grease an 8-inch cast-iron skillet, and heat in oven 5 minutes.

2. Meanwhile, whisk together first 5 ingredients in a bowl; whisk in melted butter. Add eggs and buttermilk, whisking just until smooth.

3. Pour batter into hot skillet. Bake at 400° for 30 to 33 minutes or until golden brown.

Sour Cream Cornbread

Sweet Endings

*The tempting aromas of holiday goodies
wafting from the kitchen are the source
of many fond Christmas memories.*

Snowy Chocolate Baby Cakes

MAKES: about 24 servings   ✳   **HANDS-ON TIME:** 45 min.   ✳   **TOTAL TIME:** 1 hr., 50 min., including glaze

During testing, we found that muffin cups range from 2½ to 3 oz. each. The size you have will determine your yield.

1	(18.25-oz.) package devil's food cake mix	2	large eggs
1	(16-oz.) container sour cream	1	tsp. vanilla extract
½	cup milk		Winter White Glaze
¼	cup butter, melted		Garnishes: red cinnamon candies, fresh mint leaves*

1. Preheat oven to 350°. Beat first 6 ingredients at low speed with an electric mixer just until dry ingredients are moistened. Increase speed to medium, and beat 1 to 2 minutes or until smooth, stopping to scrape down sides of bowl as needed. Spoon batter into 2 greased and floured (12-cup) muffin pans.

2. Bake at 350° for 20 to 22 minutes or until a wooden pick inserted in center comes out clean. Cool in pans 5 minutes. Remove from pans to wire racks, and cool completely (about 30 minutes).

3. Arrange cakes upside down on a serving platter. Spoon Winter White Glaze over cakes (about 1 Tbsp. per cake), spreading with a spatula to thoroughly cover cakes. Garnish, if desired.

*Fresh bay leaves may be substituted.

Note: We tested with Duncan Hines Moist Deluxe Devil's Food Premium Cake Mix.

Winter White Glaze

MAKES: about 2 cups   ✳   **HANDS-ON TIME:** 10 min.   ✳   **TOTAL TIME:** 10 min.

Cover glaze surface directly with a damp paper towel, as needed, to prevent a crust from forming before you've finished icing the cupcakes.

4	cups powdered sugar	¼	cup hot water
1	Tbsp. meringue powder		

1. Beat all ingredients with an electric mixer until smooth. Use immediately.

Lemon-Poppy Seed Cakes

MAKES: 18 mini Bundt cakes ❋ **HANDS-ON TIME:** 25 min. ❋ **TOTAL TIME:** 1 hr.

Miniature Bundt pans (not to be confused with smaller Bundt pans) look like regular muffin pans; however, they have Bundt-shaped cups. The cups in mini Bundt pans can vary in size and shape, so your yield can also vary. For this recipe, we used two pans.

½	cup butter, softened		2	tsp. lemon zest, divided
2	oz. cream cheese, softened		1¾	cups all-purpose flour
1¼	cups granulated sugar		¾	tsp. baking powder
2	large eggs		⅛	tsp. salt
¾	cup milk		1¼	cups powdered sugar
¾	tsp. poppy seeds		¼	cup fresh lemon juice
¾	tsp. almond extract			

1. Preheat oven to 350°. Beat butter and cream cheese at medium speed with an electric mixer until well blended. Gradually add granulated sugar, beating until creamy and fluffy. Add eggs, 1 at a time, beating just until yellow disappears after each addition. Beat in milk, poppy seeds, almond extract, and 1½ tsp. lemon zest. (Mixture will be slightly lumpy.)

2. Whisk together flour and next 2 ingredients in a large bowl. Gradually add to butter mixture, beating until blended. Spoon batter into 1 greased and floured (12-cup) miniature Bundt pan, filling all cups three-fourths full. Spoon remaining batter into second pan, filling only 6 cups.

3. Bake at 350° for 24 to 26 minutes or until a wooden pick inserted in center comes out clean. Remove from pans to wire racks, and cool cakes 10 minutes.

4. Whisk together powdered sugar, lemon juice, and remaining ½ tsp. lemon zest until smooth. Drizzle glaze over warm cakes. Let cakes stand 4 to 5 minutes or until glaze sets.

Basic White Cupcakes

MAKES: 2 dozen ❋ **HANDS-ON TIME:** 20 min. ❋ **TOTAL TIME:** 2 hr., including buttercream

1 (18.25-oz.) package white cake mix with pudding	Paper baking cups
1¼ cups buttermilk	Vegetable cooking spray
¼ cup butter, melted	Vanilla Buttercream
2 large eggs	Toppings: assorted candy-coated pieces, sprinkles, jelly beans
2 tsp. vanilla extract	
½ tsp. almond extract	

1. Preheat oven to 350°. Beat first 6 ingredients at low speed with an electric mixer just until dry ingredients are moistened. Increase speed to medium, and beat 2 minutes or until batter is smooth, stopping to scrape down sides of bowl as needed.

2. Place paper baking cups in 2 (24-cup) muffin pans. Coat with cooking spray. Spoon batter into baking cups, filling two-thirds full.

3. Bake at 350° for 20 to 25 minutes or until a wooden pick inserted in centers comes out clean. Cool in pans on wire racks 10 minutes; remove from pans to wire racks, and cool completely (about 1 hour). Pipe Vanilla Buttercream onto cupcakes, and sprinkle with desired toppings.

Note: We tested with Pillsbury Moist Supreme Classic White Premium Cake Mix.

Vanilla Buttercream

MAKES: 3 cups ❋ **HANDS-ON TIME:** 10 min. ❋ **TOTAL TIME:** 10 min.

½ cup butter, softened	¼ cup milk
1 (3-oz.) package cream cheese, softened	1 tsp. vanilla extract
1 (16-oz.) package powdered sugar	

1. Beat butter and cream cheese at medium speed with an electric mixer until creamy. Gradually add sugar, beating at low speed until blended. Slowly beat in milk and vanilla. Increase speed to medium, and beat until smooth. Pipe onto cupcakes.

TRY THIS TWIST!

Chocolate Buttercream: Microwave 1 cup dark chocolate morsels in a microwave-safe bowl at MEDIUM (50% power) for 1½ to 2 minutes or until melted and smooth, stirring at 30-second intervals. Gradually add melted chocolate to Vanilla Buttercream; beat until smooth.

Note: We tested with Hershey's Special Dark Chocolate Chips.

Black-and-White Cupcakes

MAKES: 2 dozen * **HANDS-ON TIME:** 20 min. * **TOTAL TIME:** 2 hr., including buttercream

For best texture, don't shortcut the beating time on the cake mix.

1 (18.25-oz.) package German chocolate cake mix	Paper baking cups
1 (16-oz.) container sour cream	Vegetable cooking spray
¼ cup butter, melted	Vanilla Buttercream
2 large eggs	Toppings: assorted candy-coated pieces, sprinkles, jelly beans
1 tsp. vanilla extract	

1. Preheat oven to 350°. Beat first 5 ingredients at low speed with an electric mixer just until dry ingredients are moistened. Increase speed to medium, and beat 1 to 2 minutes or until smooth, stopping to scrape down sides of bowl as needed.

2. Place paper baking cups in 2 (24-cup) muffin pans. Coat with cooking spray. Spoon batter into baking cups, filling two-thirds full.

3. Bake at 350° for 20 to 25 minutes or until a wooden pick inserted in center comes out clean. Cool in pans on wire racks 10 minutes; remove cupcakes from pans to wire racks, and cool completely (about 1 hour). Pipe Vanilla Buttercream onto cupcakes, and sprinkle with desired toppings.

Chocolate-Red Velvet Layer Cake

Fluted Chocolate-Red
Velvet Cake

Chocolate-Red Velvet Layer Cake

MAKES: 16 servings * **HANDS-ON TIME:** 30 min.
TOTAL TIME: 2 hr., 13 min., including batter and frosting

Chocolate-Red Velvet Layer Cake is big and makes an impressive statement on any holiday buffet.

1   recipe Chocolate-Red Velvet Cake Batter
1½   recipes Big Batch Cream Cheese Frosting

Garnishes: fresh mint sprigs, raspberry candies

1. Preheat oven to 350°. Spoon Chocolate-Red Velvet Cake Batter evenly into 6 greased and floured 8-inch round foil cake pans. Bake 18 to 20 minutes or until a wooden pick inserted in center comes out clean.
2. Cool in pans on wire racks 10 minutes; remove from pans to wire racks, and cool completely (about 1 hour).
3. Meanwhile, prepare 1½ recipes Big Batch Cream Cheese Frosting. Spread frosting between layers and on top and sides of cake. Garnish, if desired.

Note: We baked our cake layers in 6 (8-inch) disposable foil cake pans, so we could fill all the pans at once. This way, if you need to bake the cake layers in batches, the second batch will be ready to put in the oven as soon as the first one is done. To allow the heat to circulate for even baking, space pans at least 2 inches apart from one another and away from the inside walls of the oven. Although the pans are disposable, they can be washed and reused.

Chocolate-Red Velvet Cake Batter

MAKES: about 7 cups ✳ **HANDS-ON TIME:** 15 min. ✳ **TOTAL TIME:** 15 min.

1	cup butter, softened	¼	tsp. baking soda
2½	cups sugar	1	(8-oz.) container sour cream
6	large eggs	2	tsp. vanilla extract
3	cups all-purpose flour	2	(1-oz.) bottles red food coloring
3	Tbsp. unsweetened cocoa		

1. Beat butter at medium speed with an electric mixer until creamy. Gradually add sugar, beating until light and fluffy. Add eggs, 1 at a time, beating just until blended after each addition.

2. Stir together flour, cocoa, and baking soda. Add to butter mixture alternately with sour cream, beginning and ending with flour mixture. Beat at low speed until blended after each addition. Stir in vanilla and red food coloring. Use batter immediately.

Big Batch Cream Cheese Frosting

MAKES: about 5 cups ✳ **HANDS-ON TIME:** 15 min. ✳ **TOTAL TIME:** 15 min.

2	(8-oz.) packages cream cheese, softened	2	(16-oz.) packages powdered sugar
½	cup butter, softened	2	tsp. vanilla extract

1. Beat cream cheese and butter at medium speed with an electric mixer until creamy. Gradually add powdered sugar, beating until light and fluffy. Stir in vanilla.

TRY THIS TWIST!

Fluted Chocolate-Red Velvet Cakes: Preheat oven to 325°. Spoon Chocolate-Red Velvet Cake Batter evenly into 3 greased and floured 8-inch brioche pans. Bake 50 minutes or until a wooden pick inserted in center comes out clean. Cool in pans on wire racks 10 minutes; remove from pans to wire racks, and cool completely (about 1 hour). Meanwhile, prepare Vanilla Glaze during last 5 minutes of cakes' cooling time. Spoon glaze evenly over top of cakes. Garnish, if desired. MAKES: 3 cakes; HANDS-ON TIME: 30 min.; TOTAL TIME: 2 hr., 30 min., including batter and glaze

Vanilla Glaze: Stir together 1 (16-oz.) package powdered sugar, 5 Tbsp. milk, and 2 tsp. vanilla extract just until powdered sugar is moistened and mixture is smooth. Add an additional tablespoon of milk, if necessary, for desired consistency. Use immediately. MAKES: about 1½ cups; HANDS-ON TIME: 5 min.; TOTAL TIME: 5 min.

Note: We kept this glaze very thick so that it wouldn't drip all the way down the sides of the Fluted Chocolate-Red Velvet Cakes, but feel free to make it a little thinner if you'd like to drizzle it over other cakes.

Lightened Hummingbird Cake

MAKES: 20 servings   ✳   **HANDS-ON TIME:** 20 min.   ✳   **TOTAL TIME:** 2 hr., 13 min., including frosting

We lowered the fat and calories by substituting applesauce for some of the oil, using less butter and sugar, fewer eggs, and substituting light for regular cream cheese.

Vegetable cooking spray
3 cups plus 2 tsp. all-purpose flour, divided
1 tsp. baking soda
½ tsp. salt
1¾ cups sugar
1 tsp. ground cinnamon
2 large eggs
½ cup unsweetened applesauce
3 Tbsp. vegetable oil
5 to 6 bananas, mashed (1¾ cups)
1½ tsp. vanilla extract
1 (8-oz.) can crushed pineapple in juice, undrained
Lightened Cream Cheese Frosting
Garnishes: orange rind curls, pecan halves

1. Preheat oven to 350°. Coat 3 (9-inch) round cake pans with cooking spray; sprinkle 2 tsp. flour into pans, shaking to coat.

2. Combine remaining 3 cups flour and next 4 ingredients in a large bowl. Stir together eggs and next 2 ingredients; add to flour mixture, stirring just until dry ingredients are moistened. (Do not beat.) Stir in mashed bananas and next 2 ingredients. Pour batter into prepared pans.

3. Bake at 350° for 23 to 25 minutes or until a wooden pick inserted in center comes out clean. Cool layers in pans on wire racks 10 minutes; remove layers to wire racks, and cool completely (about 1 hour).

4. Meanwhile, prepare Lightened Cream Cheese Frosting. Spread frosting between layers and on top and sides of cake. Garnish, if desired.

Lightened Cream Cheese Frosting

MAKES: 3½ cups   ✳   **HANDS-ON TIME:** 10 min.   ✳   **TOTAL TIME:** 20 min.

¾ cup chopped pecans
1 (8-oz.) package ⅓-less-fat cream cheese (unsoftened)
1 (3-oz.) package cream cheese, softened
1 Tbsp. light butter, unsoftened
6 cups powdered sugar
1 tsp. vanilla extract

1. Preheat oven to 350°. Bake pecans in a single layer in a shallow pan 10 to 12 minutes or until lightly toasted and fragrant, stirring halfway through. Cool.

2. Beat cream cheeses and butter at high speed with an electric mixer until creamy. Gradually add powdered sugar, beating at low speed just until smooth. Stir in vanilla and pecans.

Sugar-and-Spice Cake

MAKES: 12 servings ✳ **HANDS-ON TIME:** 1 hr. ✳ **TOTAL TIME:** 3 hr., 35 min., including frosting

1   (18.25-oz.) package white cake mix
1   (16-oz.) container sour cream
¼   cup butter, melted
2   large eggs
2   tsp. apple pie spice
1   tsp. vanilla extract

½   tsp. almond extract (optional)
Cream Cheese Frosting
Garnishes: sparkling sugar, clear edible glitter, rosemary sprigs, pecan halves, cranberries

1. Preheat oven to 350°. Beat together first 6 ingredients and, if desired, almond extract at low speed with an electric mixer just until dry ingredients are moistened. Increase speed to medium, and beat 2 minutes or until batter is smooth, stopping to scrape sides of bowl as needed. Pour batter into 3 greased and floured 8-inch round cake pans.

2. Bake at 350° for 20 to 22 minutes or until a wooden pick inserted in center comes out clean. Cool in pans on wire racks 5 minutes; remove from pans to wire racks, and cool completely (about 1 hour). Wrap in plastic wrap, and freeze 1 hour or up to 1 month.

3. Spread Cream Cheese Frosting between layers and on top and sides of cake. Garnish, if desired.

Note: We tested with Duncan Hines Moist Deluxe Classic White Cake Premium Cake Mix.

Cream Cheese Frosting

MAKES: about 6 cups ✳ **HANDS-ON TIME:** 10 min. ✳ **TOTAL TIME:** 10 min.

1   (8-oz.) package cream cheese, softened
1   cup butter, softened
2   (16-oz.) packages powdered sugar

1   Tbsp. milk
1   tsp. vanilla extract
¼   tsp. salt

1. Beat cream cheese and butter at medium speed with an electric mixer until creamy. Gradually add powdered sugar and next 3 ingredients, beating at low speed just until blended. Increase speed to medium, and beat until well blended and smooth.

Fresh Apple Cake

MAKES: 12 to 15 servings ✳ **HANDS-ON TIME:** 25 min. ✳ **TOTAL TIME:** 2 hr., not including frosting

1½ cups chopped pecans
½ cup butter, melted
2 cups sugar
2 large eggs
1 tsp. vanilla extract
2 cups all-purpose flour
2 tsp. ground cinnamon
1 tsp. baking soda
1 tsp. salt
2½ lb. Granny Smith apples (about 4 large), peeled and cut into ¼-inch-thick wedges
Fluffy Cream Cheese Frosting, Browned Butter Frosting

1. Preheat oven to 350°. Bake pecans in a single layer in a shallow pan 5 to 7 minutes or until lightly toasted and fragrant, stirring halfway through. Stir together butter and next 3 ingredients in a large bowl until blended.
2. Combine flour and next 3 ingredients; add to butter mixture, stirring until blended. Stir in apple wedges and 1 cup pecans. (Batter will be very thick, similar to a cookie dough.) Spread batter into a lightly greased 13- x 9-inch pan.
3. Bake at 350° for 45 minutes or until a wooden pick inserted in center comes out clean. Cool completely in pan on a wire rack (about 45 minutes). Spread your choice of frosting over top of cake; sprinkle with remaining ½ cup pecans.

Fluffy Cream Cheese Frosting

MAKES: about 1⅔ cups ✳ **HANDS-ON TIME:** 10 min. ✳ **TOTAL TIME:** 10 min.

1 (8-oz.) package cream cheese, softened
3 Tbsp. butter, softened
1½ cups powdered sugar
⅛ tsp. salt
1 tsp. vanilla extract

1. Beat cream cheese and butter at medium speed with an electric mixer until creamy. Gradually add powdered sugar and salt, beating until blended. Stir in vanilla.

Browned Butter Frosting

MAKES: about 3½ cups ✳ **HANDS-ON TIME:** 16 min. ✳ **TOTAL TIME:** 1 hr., 16 min.

1 cup butter
1 (16-oz.) package powdered sugar
¼ cup milk
1 tsp. vanilla extract

1. Cook butter in a small heavy saucepan over medium heat, stirring constantly, 6 to 8 minutes or until butter begins to turn golden brown. Remove pan from heat immediately, and pour butter into a small bowl. Cover and chill 1 hour or until butter cools and begins to solidify.
2. Beat butter at medium speed with an electric mixer until fluffy; gradually add powdered sugar alternately with milk, beginning and ending with powdered sugar. Beat mixture at low speed until well blended after each addition. Stir in vanilla.

Fresh Apple Cake
with Browned Butter
Frosting

Two-Step Pound Cake

MAKES: 10 to 12 servings * **HANDS-ON TIME:** 15 min. * **TOTAL TIME:** 2 hr., 55 min.

You'll need a heavy-duty stand mixer with a 4-qt. bowl and paddle attachment.

4 cups all-purpose flour	¾ cup milk
3 cups sugar	6 large eggs
2 cups butter, softened	2 tsp. vanilla extract

1. Preheat oven to 325°. Place all ingredients in 4-qt. bowl of a heavy-duty electric stand mixer. Beat at low speed 1 minute, stopping to scrape down sides as needed. Beat at medium speed 2 minutes.

2. Pour into a greased and floured 10-inch (16-cup) tube pan, and smooth batter.

3. Bake at 325° for 1 hour and 30 minutes or until a long wooden pick inserted in center comes out clean. Cool in pan on a wire rack 10 minutes. Remove from pan to wire rack, and cool completely (about 1 hour).

test kitchen tips: pound cake pointers

■ Prepare the recipe as directed and use name-brand ingredients. Store brands of sugar are often more finely ground than name brands, yielding more sugar per cup, which can cause the cake to fall. Store brands of butter can contain more liquid fat or flours more hard wheat, making the cake heavy.

■ Measure accurately. Extra sugar or leavening causes a cake to fall; extra flour makes it dry.

■ Add the eggs 1 at a time, beating just until the yellow yolk disappears. Overbeating the eggs can cause the batter to overflow the sides of the pan when baked or create a fragile crust that crumbles and separates from the cake as it cools.

■ Test for doneness by inserting a long wooden pick into the center of the cake. It should come out clean, with no batter or wet crumbs clinging to it. (Some cakes will have a crack in the center that appears "wet," even when fully cooked, so try to avoid this area when testing.)

■ After removing from the oven, place the pound cake right side up in the pan on a wire rack and cool for 10 minutes, away from drafts. This allows the cake to become firm enough to remove from the pan without breaking apart. Cooling too long in the pan will cause the cake to become damp and stick to the pan.

Chocolate-Coffee Cheesecake

MAKES: 8 servings ✳ **HANDS-ON TIME:** 20 min. ✳ **TOTAL TIME:** 9 hr., 50 min.

1 (10-oz.) box chocolate-flavored bear-shaped graham crackers, crushed (about 2¼ cups)
6 Tbsp. butter, melted
1 cup plus 2 Tbsp. sugar, divided
4 (8-oz.) packages cream cheese, softened
¼ cup plus 1 Tbsp. coffee liqueur, divided

1 tsp. instant coffee granules
1 tsp. vanilla extract
4 large eggs
4 (1-oz.) bittersweet baking chocolate squares
1 (16-oz.) container sour cream
Garnishes: blackberries, currants, strawberries

1. Preheat oven to 350°. Stir together crushed graham crackers, butter, and 1 Tbsp. sugar. Press mixture on bottom and halfway up sides of a 9-inch springform pan. Bake at 350° for 10 minutes. Cool crust in pan on a wire rack. Reduce oven temperature to 325°.

2. Beat cream cheese and 1 cup sugar at medium speed with an electric mixer until blended. Add ¼ cup coffee liqueur, coffee granules, and vanilla, beating at low speed until well blended. Add eggs, 1 at a time, beating just until yellow disappears after each addition.

3. Remove and reserve 1 cup cream cheese mixture. Pour remaining batter into prepared crust.

4. Microwave chocolate squares in a medium-size glass bowl at HIGH 1 minute or until melted, stirring at 30-second intervals; cool slightly. Stir reserved 1 cup cream cheese mixture into melted chocolate, blending well. Spoon chocolate mixture in lines on top of batter in springform pan; gently swirl with a knife.

5. Bake at 325° for 1 hour or until almost set. Turn oven off. Let cheesecake stand in oven, with door closed, 30 minutes. Remove cheesecake from oven, and gently run a knife around outer edge of cheesecake to loosen from sides of pan. (Do not remove sides of pan.) Stir together sour cream, remaining 1 Tbsp. sugar, and remaining 1 Tbsp. coffee liqueur. Spread sour cream mixture over cheesecake. Cool on a wire rack. Cover and chill at least 8 hours. Garnish, if desired.

test kitchen tips: cheesecake cracks

Some cracks in cheesecakes are normal and can even make them look prettier.

1. Generally the more slowly the cheesecake is cooked, the less chance there is for cracking. Use an oven thermometer to make sure your oven stays at the correct temperature.

2. After the cheesecake has cooled in the oven, remove it, and run a knife around the edge. Cool completely on a wire rack; then cover and chill at least 8 hours.

Individual Frozen Peppermint Cheesecakes

MAKES: 18 cheesecakes ✳ **HANDS-ON TIME:** 25 min. ✳ **TOTAL TIME:** 2 hr., 25 min.

Peppermint ice-cream lovers, this one's for you! These melt fast, so serve them quickly.

18 vanilla wafers
18 aluminum foil baking cups
1 (8-oz.) package cream cheese, softened
1 (14-oz.) can sweetened condensed milk
1 cup crushed hard peppermint candy

3 drops red liquid food coloring
1 (8-oz.) container frozen whipped topping, thawed and divided
Garnish: crushed hard peppermint candy

1. Place 1 vanilla wafer in each aluminum foil baking cup or paper-lined muffin cup.

2. Beat cream cheese at high speed with an electric mixer until creamy. Stir in condensed milk, crushed candy, and food coloring. Fold in 2 cups whipped topping.

3. Spoon peppermint mixture evenly into muffin cups; cover and freeze 2 hours or until firm. Dollop or pipe remaining 1 cup whipped topping evenly on tops of frozen cheesecakes. Garnish, if desired.

> **TRY THIS TWIST!**

Frozen Peppermint Cheesecake: Stir together 40 finely crushed vanilla wafers, ¼ cup powdered sugar, and ¼ cup melted butter; firmly press on bottom and 1 inch up sides of a 9-inch springform pan. Freeze 15 minutes. Proceed as directed through Step 2. Pour peppermint mixture into prepared crust. Cover and freeze 4 hours. Spread remaining 1 cup whipped topping over cheesecake. Garnish, if desired. MAKES: 10 servings; HANDS-ON TIME: 25 min.; TOTAL TIME: 4 hr., 40 min.

test kitchen tip: how to use cupcake liners

■ Paper liners can be a fun way to add color and interest to your cupcakes, but their purpose is also functional—they keep these sweet treats from sticking to the pan and also make cleanup quick and easy. If you're using liners, there's no need to coat the pan with cooking spray, but you should coat the liners with cooking spray to make them easier to peel off.

Charlotte Russe

MAKES: 12 servings ❊ **HANDS-ON TIME:** 30 min. ❊ **TOTAL TIME:** 8 hr., 30 min.

2 (0.7-oz.) envelopes unflavored gelatin
½ cup cold water
7 egg yolks
1 cup granulated sugar
2 cups milk
¼ cup almond liqueur or ½ tsp. almond extract

2 tsp. vanilla extract
4 cups frozen whipped topping, thawed
2 (3-oz.) packages ladyfingers
2 pt. fresh raspberries
¼ cup sifted powdered sugar

1. Sprinkle gelatin over ½ cup cold water; let stand 1 minute.

2. Beat egg yolks and sugar in a heavy saucepan at medium speed with an electric mixer 3 to 4 minutes or until thick and pale.

3. Heat milk over low heat; add to egg mixture in a slow, steady stream, whisking constantly. Cook over low heat, whisking constantly, 5 to 7 minutes or until mixture coats a spoon. Remove from heat; add gelatin mixture, stirring until gelatin dissolves. Stir in liqueur and vanilla, and pour into a metal bowl. Place bowl in a larger bowl of ice, and let stand, stirring often, 8 to 10 minutes or until slightly thickened.

4. Fold whipped topping gently into custard.

5. Line a plastic wrap-lined 9-inch springform pan with ladyfingers, placing rounded sides against bottom and sides of pan. Pour in custard mixture; chill 8 hours. Remove sides from pan. Grasping edges of plastic wrap, transfer charlotte to a serving plate. Trim one side of plastic wrap. Lift charlotte with a spatula, and remove plastic wrap. Cover top with fresh raspberries, and sprinkle with powdered sugar.

Red Velvet Trifle

MAKES: 10 servings ✳ **HANDS-ON TIME:** 25 min. ✳ **TOTAL TIME:** 3 hr.

1 (18.25-oz.) package moist red velvet cake mix
2 (8-oz.) packages cream cheese, softened
2 cups low-fat vanilla yogurt

1 cup powdered sugar
1 tsp. lemon zest
1 pt. fresh raspberries
Garnish: fresh mint sprigs

1. Preheat oven to 350°. Prepare cake batter as directed. Pour batter into a greased and floured 13- x 9-inch pan.

2. Bake at 350° for 28 to 30 minutes or until a wooden pick inserted in center comes out clean.

3. Meanwhile, beat cream cheese at medium speed with a heavy-duty electric stand mixer 1 minute or until creamy. Add yogurt and next 2 ingredients. Beat 1 to 2 minutes or until smooth, stopping to scrape down sides of bowl as needed. Cover and chill.

4. Remove cake from oven. Cool in pan on a wire rack 10 minutes. Remove from pan to a wire rack, and cool completely (about 1 hour).

5. Invert cake onto a cutting board. Cut rounded top off of cake. Trim and discard edges of cake. Cut cake into 32 pieces.

6. Arrange about one-third of cake pieces in a 3-qt. trifle dish. Carefully spread one-third of chilled cream cheese mixture over cake. Repeat layers 2 times, smoothing top layer of cream cheese mixture over cake pieces. Top with raspberries. Cover and chill 1 hour before serving. Garnish, if desired.

Note: We tested with Duncan Hines Moist Deluxe Red Velvet Premium Cake Mix.

Enjoy this decadent twist on a Christmas classic— a trifle boasting the flavors of red velvet cake, cream cheese, and fresh raspberries.

Chocolate-Cranberry Roulade

MAKES: 6 to 8 servings ❊ **HANDS-ON TIME:** 25 min.
TOTAL TIME: 3 hr., 50 min., including filling

Roulade, a classic rolled-cake dessert, resembles a jelly roll. This recipe makes two cakes. Freeze one for later use.

Vegetable cooking spray
Parchment paper
Unsweetened cocoa
4 large eggs

1 (18.25- or 18.5-oz.) package Swiss chocolate, devil's food, or fudge cake mix
Cranberry Filling
Garnish: holly leaves and berries

1. Preheat oven to 350°. Coat 2 (15- x 10- x 1-inch) jelly-roll pans with cooking spray; line with parchment paper. Coat again with cooking spray, and dust with cocoa, shaking out excess.
2. Beat eggs in a large mixing bowl at medium-high speed with an electric mixer 5 minutes. Add ½ cup water, beating at low speed just until blended. Gradually add cake mix, beating until moistened; beat at medium-high speed 2 minutes. Divide batter in half, and spread into prepared pans. (Layers will be thin.)
3. Bake each cake at 350° on middle oven rack (in separate ovens) for 10 minutes or until cake springs back when lightly touched in center. (If you don't have a double oven, set 1 pan aside.)
4. Remove cakes from ovens, and immediately loosen from sides of pans. Turn out onto cloth towels dusted with cocoa. Peel off parchment paper. While cakes are warm, roll up each cake and towel together, beginning at narrow end. Place, seam side down, on wire racks, and cool completely (about 1 hour). Gently unroll cooled cakes, and spread with Cranberry Filling. Reroll cakes without towel; cover and freeze at least 1 hour.
5. Dust each cake with cocoa just before serving, and cut into 1- to 2-inch slices. Serve with reserved cranberry mixture. Garnish, if desired.

Cranberry Filling

MAKES: 2 cups ❊ **HANDS-ON TIME:** 15 min. ❊ **TOTAL TIME:** 1 hr., 15 min.

1 (12-oz.) container cranberry-raspberry relish or cranberry-orange relish
1 cup cranberry juice cocktail

2 Tbsp. powdered sugar
1½ Tbsp. cornstarch
2 cups whipping cream

1. Process first 4 ingredients in a blender or food processor until smooth, stopping several times to scrape down sides.
2. Pour mixture into a small saucepan; bring to a boil over medium heat, stirring constantly. Boil, stirring constantly, 1 minute. Remove from heat, and let stand 1 hour or until completely cool.
3. Beat cream at medium speed with an electric mixer until soft peaks form. Fold in ⅔ cup cranberry mixture; cover and chill remaining cranberry mixture.

Caramel-Pecan-Pumpkin Bread Puddings

MAKES: 11 servings ✳ **HANDS-ON TIME:** 27 min. ✳ **TOTAL TIME:** 9 hr., 27 min.

BREAD PUDDINGS:
- 4 large eggs
- 2 (15-oz.) cans pumpkin
- 1½ cups milk
- 1 cup half-and-half
- 1 cup granulated sugar
- 1 tsp. ground cinnamon
- ½ tsp. salt
- ½ tsp. ground nutmeg
- ½ tsp. vanilla extract
- 1 (12-oz.) French bread loaf, cut into 1-inch pieces (about 10 cups)

CARAMEL-PECAN SAUCE:
- 1 cup pecans, chopped
- 1 cup firmly packed light brown sugar
- ½ cup butter
- 1 Tbsp. light corn syrup
- 1 tsp. vanilla extract

1. Prepare Bread Puddings: Whisk together eggs and next 8 ingredients in a large bowl until well blended. Add bread pieces, stirring to thoroughly coat. Cover with plastic wrap, and chill 8 to 24 hours.

2. Preheat oven to 350°. Spoon bread mixture into 11 (6-oz.) lightly greased ramekins. (Ramekins will be completely full, and mixture will mound slightly.) Place on an aluminum foil-lined jelly-roll pan.

3. Bake at 350° for 50 minutes, shielding with foil after 30 minutes.

4. During last 15 minutes of baking, prepare Caramel-Pecan Sauce: Heat pecans in a medium skillet over medium-low heat, stirring often, 3 to 5 minutes or until lightly toasted and fragrant.

5. Cook brown sugar, butter, and corn syrup in a small saucepan over medium heat, stirring occasionally, 3 to 4 minutes or until sugar dissolves. Remove from heat; stir in vanilla and pecans.

6. Remove bread puddings from oven; drizzle with Caramel-Pecan Sauce. Bake 5 minutes or until sauce is thoroughly heated and begins to bubble.

TRY THIS TWIST!

One-Dish Caramel-Pecan-Pumpkin Bread Pudding: Prepare recipe as directed in Step 1. Spoon chilled bread mixture into a lightly greased 13- x 9-inch baking dish. Cover with aluminum foil. Bake, covered, at 350° for 35 minutes. Uncover and bake 15 minutes. Proceed with recipe as directed in Steps 4 through 6.

Berry Bread Puddings

MAKES: 6 servings ✻ **HANDS-ON TIME:** 20 min. ✻ **TOTAL TIME:** 4 hr., including sauce

½ (16-oz.) Italian bread loaf, cut into
   1-inch pieces (about 6 cups)
3 large eggs
1¼ cups 2% reduced-fat milk
1 (12-oz.) can fat-free evaporated milk

¼ cup sugar
½ tsp. almond extract
6 Tbsp. seedless raspberry preserves
Raspberry Sauce

1. Place bread in 6 (8-oz.) lightly greased oval-shaped cast-iron baking dishes.

2. Whisk together eggs and next 4 ingredients; pour over bread in baking dishes (about ⅔ cup egg mixture each). Dot top of each with 1 Tbsp. preserves. Cover and chill 2 to 3 hours.

3. Preheat oven to 350°. Remove baking dishes from refrigerator, and let stand 15 minutes. Bake at 350° for 38 to 40 minutes or until tops are crisp and golden brown. Let stand 10 minutes. Serve with Raspberry Sauce.

> **TRY THIS TWIST!**

One-Dish Berry Bread Pudding: Place bread in a lightly greased 11- x 7-inch baking dish. Proceed with recipe as directed in Step 2, dotting top of bread mixture with all 6 Tbsp. raspberry preserves. Bake at 350° for 45 to 50 minutes or until top is crisp and golden brown. Let stand 10 minutes. Serve with sauce. MAKES: 6 servings; HANDS-ON TIME: 15 min.; TOTAL TIME: 3 hr., 25 min.

Raspberry Sauce

MAKES: about 1⅔ cups ✻ **HANDS-ON TIME:** 5 min. ✻ **TOTAL TIME:** 35 min.

1 (12-oz.) package frozen unsweetened
   raspberries, thawed

⅔ cup sugar
¼ cup orange juice

1. Reserve 1 cup raspberries. Process remaining berries, sugar, and orange juice in a food processor until smooth. Pour raspberry mixture through a fine wire-mesh strainer into a bowl; discard pulp and seeds. Stir in 1 cup reserved raspberries. Cover and chill 30 minutes.

> **TRY THIS TWIST!**

Reduced-Sugar Bread Pudding and Reduced-Sugar Raspberry Sauce: Prepare Berry Bread Pudding and Raspberry Sauce as directed, substituting Whey Low Granular for sugar in each.

Note: Whey Low® sweeteners offer a great-tasting reduced-sugar option. You can find them at Whole Foods Market, or order online at wheylow.com.

Chocolate-Peppermint Puddings

MAKES: 6 servings ❋ **HANDS-ON TIME:** 30 min. ❋ **TOTAL TIME:** 3 hr., 30 min.

2   cups whipping cream, divided
2   large eggs
2   egg yolks
¼   cup sugar
6   (1-oz.) semisweet chocolate baking squares, melted
3   Tbsp. coffee-flavored liqueur or strong brewed coffee

½   tsp. peppermint extract
½   cup cream-filled chocolate sandwich cookie crumbs
Garnishes: fresh mint sprigs, crushed hard peppermint candy, cream-filled chocolate sandwich cookie pieces

1. Whisk together 1 cup whipping cream, eggs, egg yolks, and sugar in a small heavy saucepan until blended. Cook over medium-low heat, whisking constantly, 10 to 12 minutes or until mixture reaches 160°. Remove from heat; pour through a wire-mesh strainer into a bowl.

2. Whisk in melted chocolate, liqueur, and peppermint extract. Cover and chill 3 hours.

3. Beat remaining 1 cup whipping cream at medium speed with an electric mixer until soft peaks form.

4. Spoon cookie crumbs on bottoms of 6 (6-oz.) bowls; top with chocolate mixture and whipped cream. Garnish, if desired.

test kitchen tips: how to make great pudding

Preparing stove-top pudding requires little more than a heavy saucepan, whisk, rubber spatula, and plastic wrap.

1. The pudding is thick enough when it coats the back of a spoon.

2. Place plastic wrap directly on the surface of the pudding to prevent a thin, rubbery skin from developing on top.

Sherry-Baked Winter Fruit

MAKES: 6 to 8 servings ✳ **HANDS-ON TIME:** 15 min.
TOTAL TIME: 13 hr., 15 min., not including cream

You can find apple cider with either shelf-stable or refrigerated juices. It doesn't matter which one you choose, so select the best value. Use dry sherry, not the much sweeter cream sherry.

1 (10-oz.) package dried Mission figlets, trimmed and halved
1 (7-oz.) package dried apricots
1 (5-oz.) package dried apples
2 cups apple cider
⅔ cup dry sherry

½ cup golden raisins
2 navel oranges, peeled and sectioned
1 (3-inch) cinnamon stick
Brown Sugar-Lemon Sour Cream (optional)
Garnish: orange slices

1. Place first 8 ingredients in an 11- x 7-inch baking dish; gently toss to combine. Cover with aluminum foil, and chill 12 to 24 hours.

2. Preheat oven to 350°. Bake fruit, covered, 45 to 50 minutes or until thoroughly heated and fruit is soft.

3. Let stand, covered, 15 minutes. Remove and discard cinnamon stick. Serve with a slotted spoon and, if desired, Brown Sugar-Lemon Sour Cream. Garnish, if desired.

TRY THESE TWISTS!

Port-Baked Winter Fruit: Substitute port for sherry. Proceed with recipe as directed.

Simple Baked Winter Fruit: Substitute 1 (12-oz.) can thawed apple juice concentrate and 1 cup water for apple cider and sherry. Proceed with recipe as directed.

Tropical Plum Sherry-Baked Winter Fruit: Substitute 1 (10-oz.) package dried pitted plums, 1 (6-oz.) package dried pineapple, and 1 (5-oz.) package dried mango, chopped, for figlets, apricots, and apples. Proceed with recipe as directed.

Brown Sugar-Lemon Sour Cream

MAKES: about 1 cup ✳ **HANDS-ON TIME:** 5 min. ✳ **TOTAL TIME:** 35 min.

This quick sauce is also delicious when served over fresh berries or granola or dolloped on pound cake.

1 (8-oz.) container sour cream
2 Tbsp. brown sugar

1 tsp. lemon zest
1 tsp. vanilla extract

1. Stir together all ingredients. Cover and chill 30 minutes or up to 48 hours.

TRY THIS TWIST!

Lightened Brown Sugar-Lemon Sour Cream: Substitute 1 (8-oz.) container reduced-fat sour cream for regular. Proceed with recipe as directed.

Sherry-Baked
Winter Fruit

Apple Upside-Down Pie

MAKES: 8 servings ✴ **HANDS-ON TIME:** 25 min. ✴ **TOTAL TIME:** 2 hr., 35 min.

1   cup chopped pecans
½   cup firmly packed light brown sugar
⅓   cup butter, melted
1   (14.1-oz.) package refrigerated piecrusts, divided
4   medium-size Granny Smith apples, peeled and cut into 1-inch chunks (about 1¾ lb.)

2   large Jonagold apples, peeled and cut into 1-inch chunks (about 1¼ lb.)
¼   cup granulated sugar
2   Tbsp. all-purpose flour
1   tsp. ground cinnamon
½   tsp. ground nutmeg

1. Preheat oven to 375°. Stir together first 3 ingredients, and spread on bottom of a 9-inch pie plate. Fit 1 piecrust over pecan mixture in pie plate, allowing excess crust to hang over sides.

2. Stir together Granny Smith apple chunks and next 5 ingredients. Spoon mixture into crust, packing tightly and mounding in center. Place remaining piecrust over filling; press both crusts together, fold edges under, and crimp. Place pie on an aluminum foil-lined jelly-roll pan. Cut 4 to 5 slits in top of pie for steam to escape.

3. Bake at 375° on lower oven rack 1 hour to 1 hour and 5 minutes or until juices are thick and bubbly, crust is golden brown, and apples are tender when pierced with a long wooden pick through slits in crust. Shield pie with aluminum foil after 50 minutes, if necessary, to prevent excessive browning. Cool on a wire rack 10 minutes. Place a serving plate over top of pie; invert pie onto serving plate. Remove pie plate, and replace any remaining pecans in pie plate on top of pie. Cool completely (about 1 hour).

test kitchen tips: how to slice and peel an apple

Be sure to peel apples just before using them because they can start to turn brown quickly.

1. Use an apple corer to remove the stem, tough center, and seeds and either a vegetable peeler or sharp pairing knife to carefully remove the peel, leaving behind as much of the flesh as possible.

2. Stand the cored, peeled apple upright, and slice vertically in half. For slices or wedges, place halves, cut sides down, and cut toward the core to make slices as thick or as thin as you like.

Peppermint Candy
Ice-Cream Pie

Peppermint Candy Ice-Cream Pie

MAKES: 8 servings ✳ **HANDS-ON TIME:** 30 min. ✳ **TOTAL TIME:** 4 hr., 30 min.

16   cream-filled chocolate sandwich cookies, finely crushed
¼   cup butter, melted
1   pt. vanilla ice cream

1   (8-oz.) container frozen whipped topping, partially thawed
12   peppermint candies, crushed
Garnish: chopped peppermint candies

1. Stir together chocolate crumbs and melted butter; press firmly into a 9-inch pie plate.
2. Combine ice cream, half of whipped topping, and crushed candies. Spoon mixture into prepared pie plate; cover and freeze 4 hours. Dollop each serving with remaining whipped topping. Garnish, if desired.

Note: We tested with Oreo cookies.

Pecan-Chocolate Chip Pie

MAKES: 8 servings ✳ **HANDS-ON TIME:** 25 min. ✳ **TOTAL TIME:** 1 hr., 25 min.

This is a marvelously rich, chocolaty version of a Southern tradition.

1   cup chopped pecans
½   (14.1-oz.) package refrigerated piecrusts
2   large eggs
½   cup all-purpose flour

½   cup granulated sugar
½   cup firmly packed light brown sugar
¾   cup butter, melted and cooled
1   cup semisweet chocolate morsels

1. Preheat oven to 350°. Bake pecans in a single layer in a shallow pan 10 to 12 minutes or until lightly toasted and fragrant, stirring halfway through. Cool. Reduce oven temperature to 325°.
2. Fit piecrust into a 9-inch pie plate according to package directions; fold edges under, and crimp.
3. Whisk eggs in a bowl until foamy. Combine flour and sugars; add to eggs, stirring until blended. Stir in butter, chocolate morsels, and toasted pecans. Pour mixture into prepared crust.
4. Bake at 325° for 1 hour or until set.

Walnut Fudge Pie

MAKES: 6 to 8 servings ✳ **HANDS-ON TIME:** 15 min. ✳ **TOTAL TIME:** 2 hr.

3 large eggs, lightly beaten
½ cup firmly packed brown sugar
¼ cup all-purpose flour
¼ cup butter, melted
1 tsp. vanilla extract
1 (12-oz.) package semisweet chocolate morsels, melted

1½ cups walnut halves*
½ (14.1-oz.) package refrigerated piecrusts
Vanilla ice cream
Java Chocolate Sauce (optional)

1. Preheat oven to 375°. Stir together first 5 ingredients until blended; stir in melted chocolate morsels and nuts.
2. Fit piecrust into a 9-inch pie plate according to package directions. Fold edges under, and crimp. Spoon filling into piecrust.
3. Bake at 375° for 30 minutes. Cool completely on a wire rack (about 1 hour). Serve with ice cream and, if desired, Java Chocolate Sauce.

*1½ cups chopped pecans may be substituted.

Java Chocolate Sauce

MAKES: 1¼ cups ✳ **HANDS-ON TIME:** 15 min. ✳ **TOTAL TIME:** 15 min.

1 (12-oz.) package semisweet chocolate morsels
½ cup whipping cream

1 Tbsp. butter
¼ cup strong brewed coffee

1. Cook first 3 ingredients in a heavy saucepan over low heat, stirring often, until chocolate morsels and butter melt. Cook, stirring constantly, 2 to 3 minutes or until smooth. Remove from heat; stir in coffee. Serve warm.

Rich Chocolate Tart

MAKES: 12 to 16 servings ✳ **HANDS-ON TIME:** 25 min. ✳ **TOTAL TIME:** 4 hr., 5 min.

1½ cups gingersnap crumbs (about 39 cookies)
6 Tbsp. butter, melted
3 Tbsp. powdered sugar
1¾ cups heavy cream

15 oz. bittersweet chocolate, chopped*
1 tsp. vanilla extract
Garnishes: sweetened whipped cream, raspberries, fresh mint sprigs

1. Preheat oven to 350°. Stir together first 3 ingredients. Firmly press on bottom and up sides of a 9-inch tart pan. Bake 8 to 9 minutes or until fragrant. Cool on a wire rack 30 minutes.
2. Bring cream to a boil in a 3-qt. saucepan over medium-high heat.
3. Process chocolate in a food processor or blender until finely ground. With processor running, pour hot cream and vanilla through food chute in a slow, steady stream, processing until smooth, stopping to scrape down sides as needed.
4. Pour mixture into cooled crust. Chill, uncovered, 3 hours. Garnish, if desired.

*Semisweet chocolate may be substituted.

Individual Pear Tartlets

MAKES: 6 servings ✽ **HANDS-ON TIME:** 30 min. ✽ **TOTAL TIME:** 1 hr., 12 min.

12 wooden picks
3 Tbsp. all-purpose flour
½ (17.3-oz.) package frozen puff pastry sheets, thawed
Parchment paper
6 Tbsp. light brown sugar
4 Tbsp. butter, melted
1 Tbsp. fresh lemon juice
½ tsp. ground cinnamon
⅛ tsp. ground allspice
5 to 6 Bosc pears (about 10 oz. each), peeled, halved lengthwise, and cut crosswise into ⅛-inch-thick slices
Garnishes: sweetened whipped cream, freshly grated nutmeg

1. Preheat oven to 400°. Soak wooden picks in water to cover 30 minutes.
2. Meanwhile, lightly dust work surface with flour; roll out 1 sheet puff pastry to ⅛-inch thickness. Cut 6 (4-inch) rounds. Cut additional shapes, such as leaves or stars, from scraps, if desired. Transfer rounds to a parchment paper-lined jelly-roll pan. Transfer shapes to a second parchment paper-lined jelly-roll pan. Chill 10 minutes or until ready to assemble.
3. Bake rounds at 400° for 7 minutes, and set aside. (Do not prebake any additional shapes.)
4. Mix together brown sugar and next 4 ingredients in a large bowl. Carefully stir in pear slices.
5. Arrange pear slices in concentric circles on rounds. When each round is stacked about 2 inches high, insert 2 presoaked wooden picks into the top of each tartlet to secure slices. Drizzle with any remaining sugar mixture.
6. Bake tartlets and shapes at 400° for 15 minutes or until shapes are puffed and golden brown. Transfer shapes to a wire rack, and cool completely. Bake tartlets 10 more minutes or until golden brown and slightly caramelized. Transfer tarts to dessert plates. Remove wooden picks. Serve immediately with baked pastry shapes. Garnish, if desired.

By using puff pastry, we have taken much of the work out of this tasty dessert.

Elegant Citrus Tart

MAKES: 8 servings ✳ **HANDS-ON TIME:** 20 min. ✳ **TOTAL TIME:** 10 hr., 5 min., including curd

Topping our tart are Florida-grown Ruby Red grapefruit and navel oranges and the brightest red grapefruit you can buy—the Rio Star from Texas.

⅓	cup sweetened flaked coconut		¼	tsp. coconut extract
2	cups all-purpose flour			Buttery Orange Curd
⅔	cup powdered sugar		9	assorted citrus fruits, peeled and sectioned
¾	cup cold butter, cut into pieces			

1. Preheat oven to 350°. Bake coconut in a single layer in a shallow pan 4 to 5 minutes or until toasted and fragrant, stirring halfway through; cool completely (about 15 minutes).

2. Pulse coconut, flour, and powdered sugar in a food processor 3 to 4 times or until combined. Add butter and coconut extract, and pulse 5 to 6 times or until crumbly. With processor running, gradually add 3 Tbsp. water, and process until dough forms a ball and leaves sides of bowl.

3. Roll dough into a 12½- x 8-inch rectangle (about ¼ inch thick) on a lightly floured surface; press on bottom and up sides of a 12- x 9-inch tart pan with removable bottom. Trim excess dough, and discard.

4. Bake at 350° for 30 minutes. Cool completely on a wire rack (about 40 minutes).

5. Spread Buttery Orange Curd over crust. Top with citrus sections.

Note: To make a round tart, roll dough into a 10-inch circle (about ¼ inch thick) on a lightly floured surface; press on bottom and up sides of a 9-inch round tart pan with removable bottom. Trim excess dough, and discard. Bake as directed.

Buttery Orange Curd

MAKES: about 2 cups ✳ **HANDS-ON TIME**: 15 min. ✳ **TOTAL TIME**: 8 hr., 15 min.

⅔	cup sugar		3	Tbsp. butter
2½	Tbsp. cornstarch		2	tsp. orange zest
1⅓	cups orange juice			Pinch of salt
1	large egg, lightly beaten			

1. Combine sugar and cornstarch in a 3-qt. saucepan; gradually whisk in orange juice. Whisk in egg. Bring to a boil; boil, whisking constantly, 3 to 4 minutes.

2. Remove from heat; whisk in butter, zest, and salt. Place heavy-duty plastic wrap directly on curd (to prevent a film from forming), and chill 8 hours. Store leftovers in refrigerator up to 3 days.

Note: We tested with Simply Orange 100% Pure Squeezed Orange Juice.

Luscious Lemon Bars

MAKES: about 2 dozen   ✳   **HANDS-ON TIME:** 20 min.   ✳   **TOTAL TIME:** 2 hr., 5 min.

2¼   cups all-purpose flour, divided
½   cup powdered sugar
1   cup cold butter, cut into pieces
4   large eggs
2   cups granulated sugar

1   tsp. lemon zest
⅓   cup fresh lemon juice
½   teaspoon baking powder
Powdered sugar

1. Preheat oven to 350°. Line bottom and sides of a 13- x 9-inch pan with heavy-duty aluminum foil or parchment paper, allowing 2 to 3 inches to extend over sides; lightly grease foil.

2. Stir together 2 cups flour and ½ cup powdered sugar. Cut in butter using a pastry blender or fork until crumbly. Press flour mixture on bottom of prepared pan.

3. Bake at 350° for 20 to 25 minutes or until lightly browned.

4. Meanwhile, whisk eggs in a large bowl until smooth; whisk in granulated sugar, lemon zest, and lemon juice. Stir together baking powder and remaining ¼ cup flour; whisk into egg mixture. Pour mixture over hot baked crust.

5. Bake at 350° for 25 minutes or until filling is set. Cool in pan on a wire rack 30 minutes. Lift from pan, using foil sides as handles. Cool completely on a wire rack (about 30 minutes). Remove foil, and cut into bars; sprinkle with powdered sugar.

Note: To make ahead, prepare lemon bars as directed. Cover tightly, and freeze up to 1 month.

Simple Brownies with Chocolate Frosting

MAKES: 4 dozen ✳ **HANDS-ON TIME**: 15 min. ✳ **TOTAL TIME**: 1 hr., 56 min., including frosting

1½	cups coarsely chopped pecans	2	cups sugar
1	(4-oz.) unsweetened chocolate baking bar, chopped	4	large eggs
		1	cup all-purpose flour
¾	cup butter		Chocolate Frosting

1. Preheat oven to 350°. Bake pecans in a single layer in a shallow pan 6 to 8 minutes or until lightly toasted and fragrant.

2. Microwave chocolate and butter in a large microwave-safe bowl at HIGH 1 to 1½ minutes or until melted and smooth, stirring at 30-second intervals. Whisk in sugar and eggs until well blended. Stir in flour. Spread batter into a greased 13- x 9-inch pan.

3. Bake at 350° for 25 to 30 minutes or until a wooden pick inserted in center comes out with a few moist crumbs.

4. Prepare Chocolate Frosting. Pour over warm brownies; spread to edges. Sprinkle with pecans. Let cool 1 hour on a wire rack. Cut into squares.

Chocolate Frosting

MAKES: 2 cups ✳ **HANDS-ON TIME**: 10 min. ✳ **TOTAL TIME**: 10 min.

½	cup butter	1	(16-oz.) package powdered sugar
⅓	cup milk	1	tsp. vanilla extract
6	Tbsp. unsweetened cocoa		

1. Cook first 3 ingredients over medium heat in a large saucepan, stirring constantly, 4 to 5 minutes or until butter melts. Remove from heat, and beat in powdered sugar and vanilla at medium speed with an electric mixer until smooth.

TRY THESE TWISTS!

Mississippi Mud Brownies: Prepare recipe through Step 3. Sprinkle brownies with pecans and 3 cups miniature marshmallows. Prepare Chocolate Frosting; pour over top. Cool 1 hour on a wire rack.

Caramel-Pecan Brownies: Prepare recipe above as directed through Step 3. Cool 1 hour on a wire rack. Combine 1 cup firmly packed dark brown sugar, ½ cup milk, 2 Tbsp. butter, and ¼ tsp. salt in a large saucepan; bring to a boil over medium-high heat, stirring occasionally. Reduce heat to medium-low, and simmer, stirring occasionally, 5 minutes or until slightly thickened. Remove from heat. Let stand 5 minutes. Beat in 1½ cups powdered sugar and ½ tsp. vanilla extract at medium speed with an electric mixer until smooth. Pour over brownies, spreading to edges; sprinkle with toasted pecans. Cool 30 minutes.

Marbled Brownies: Omit pecans and Chocolate Frosting. Preheat oven to 325°. Prepare batter as directed; spread half of batter into greased pan. Beat 1 (8-oz.) package softened cream cheese, ¼ cup sugar, 1 egg yolk, and 1 tsp. vanilla extract at medium speed with an electric mixer until smooth. Dollop cream cheese mixture over brownie batter in pan. Dollop with remaining brownie batter, and swirl together using a paring knife. Bake 35 to 40 minutes. Cool 1 hour on a wire rack.

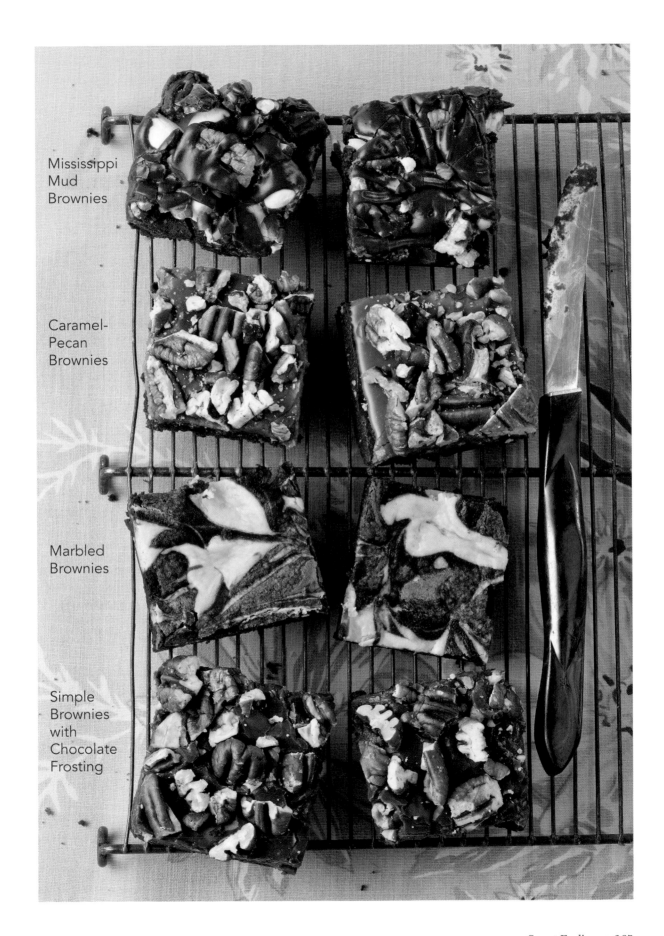

Mississippi
Mud
Brownies

Caramel-
Pecan
Brownies

Marbled
Brownies

Simple
Brownies
with
Chocolate
Frosting

Thumbprint Cookies

MAKES: 3½ dozen ❋ **HANDS-ON TIME:** 15 min. ❋ **TOTAL TIME:** 1 hr., 15 min.

1 cup butter, softened	¼ tsp. salt
¾ cup sugar	1¼ cups finely chopped pecans
2 large eggs, separated	¼ cup strawberry jam
1 tsp. almond extract	¼ cup peach jam
2 cups all-purpose flour	

1. Preheat oven to 350°. Beat butter at medium speed with an electric mixer until creamy; gradually add sugar, beating well. Add egg yolks and almond extract, beating until blended.

2. Combine flour and salt; add to butter mixture, beating at low speed until blended. Cover and chill dough 1 hour.

3. Shape dough into 1-inch balls. Lightly beat egg whites. Dip each dough ball in egg white; roll in pecans. Place 2 inches apart on ungreased baking sheets. Press thumb in each dough ball to make an indentation.

4. Bake at 350° for 15 minutes. Cool 1 minute on baking sheets, and remove to wire racks to cool completely. Press centers again with thumb while cookies are still warm; fill center of each cookie with jam.

Rosemary Shortbread Cookies

MAKES: 1½ dozen ❋ **HANDS-ON TIME:** 15 min. ❋ **TOTAL TIME:** 51 min.

1½	cups all-purpose flour	2	Tbsp. minced fresh rosemary
½	cup butter, chilled	2	Tbsp. granulated sugar
¼	cup sifted powdered sugar		

1. Preheat oven to 325°. Process first 4 ingredients in a food processor until mixture forms a ball.

2. Roll dough to ¼-inch thickness on a lightly floured surface. Cut with a 2-inch cookie cutter; place on lightly greased baking sheets.

3. Bake at 325° for 18 to 20 minutes or until edges are lightly browned. Sprinkle with granulated sugar. Remove cookies to wire racks to cool completely.

Gifts from the Kitchen

Delight everyone on your list with these tasty treats.

Cornbread
Madeleines

Anna

Cornbread Madeleines

MAKES: 4 dozen ✳ **HANDS-ON TIME:** 10 min. ✳ **TOTAL TIME:** 1 hr., 14 min.

2	cups self-rising white cornmeal mix	2	cups buttermilk
½	cup all-purpose flour	½	cup butter, melted
¼	cup sugar	2	large eggs, lightly beaten

1. Preheat oven to 400°. Whisk together cornmeal mix, flour, and sugar in a large bowl. Add buttermilk, melted butter, and eggs. Whisk together just until blended. Spoon batter into lightly greased shiny madeleine pans, filling three-fourths full.

2. Bake at 400°, in batches, 16 to 18 minutes or until golden brown. Remove from pans immediately. Serve hot, or cool completely on wire racks (about 20 minutes), and freeze in zip-top plastic freezer bags up to 1 month. To serve, arrange desired amount of madeleines on a baking sheet, and bake at 350° for 5 to 6 minutes or until thoroughly heated.

TRY THESE TWISTS!

Orange-Rosemary Cornbread Madeleines: Prepare recipe as directed, adding 2 Tbsp. orange zest and 1½ Tbsp. finely chopped fresh rosemary to dry ingredients.

Lemon-Thyme Cornbread Madeleines: Prepare recipe as directed, adding 1 Tbsp. lemon zest and 1 Tbsp. finely chopped fresh thyme to dry ingredients.

Spicy White Cheddar Cornbread Madeleines: Reduce sugar to 2 Tbsp. Prepare recipe as directed, adding ¾ cup finely shredded white Cheddar cheese and ¼ tsp. ground red pepper to dry ingredients.

Note: The traditional shiny heavy-gauge, tinned steel madeleine pan, which makes one dozen 3- x 2-inch madeleines, yields the prettiest results. (Dark nonstick versions tend to over-brown.) Look for shiny pans in bake shops, or order online from bakeandcookco.com ($17.95) or amazon.com. To prevent over-browning if you do use a dark nonstick madeleine pan, wrap the bottom of the pan with a sheet of heavy-duty aluminum foil, shiny side out.

Pimiento Cheese Cookies

MAKES: 2 dozen ✳ **HANDS-ON TIME:** 30 min. ✳ **TOTAL TIME:** 3 hr., 35 min.

1   cup all-purpose flour
1   cup refrigerated pimiento cheese
½   cup pecans, finely chopped

¼   cup butter, softened
Parchment paper
4   Tbsp. strawberry preserves

1. Beat together flour and pimiento cheese at medium speed with a heavy-duty electric stand mixer 1 minute. Add pecans and butter; beat until blended. Wrap dough in plastic wrap; chill 2 hours.

2. Preheat oven to 400°. Place dough on a well-floured surface, and roll to ⅛-inch thickness. Cut into 48 rounds with a 2-inch round cookie cutter, rerolling scraps once. Arrange half of rounds 2 inches apart on parchment paper-lined baking sheets; spoon ½ tsp. strawberry preserves onto center of each round, and top with remaining rounds, pressing edges to seal.

3. Bake at 400° for 12 to 15 minutes or until golden brown. Cool on baking sheets 10 minutes; transfer to wire racks, and cool completely (about 30 minutes).

Christmas Shortbread Cookies

MAKES: 16 (4¾-inch) cookies ✳ **HANDS-ON TIME:** 20 min. ✳ **TOTAL TIME:** 55 min.

2   cups unsalted butter, softened
4½   cups all-purpose flour

1¼   cups lightly packed light brown sugar
Pinch of salt

1. Preheat oven to 275°. Beat all ingredients at medium speed with a heavy-duty electric stand mixer just until combined.

2. Place dough on a lightly floured surface, and roll to ⅛-inch thickness. Cut with a 4¾-inch Christmas tree-shape cookie cutter. Place 1 inch apart on ungreased baking sheets.

3. Bake, in batches, at 275° for 15 minutes or until golden brown. Let cool on baking sheets 1 minute. Transfer to wire racks, and cool completely (about 5 minutes).

Pimiento Cheese
Cookies

Cinnamon-Nut Palmiers

MAKES: 5 dozen ✳ **HANDS-ON TIME:** 40 min. ✳ **TOTAL TIME:** 1 hr., 40 min.

1 (17.3-oz.) package frozen puff pastry sheets, thawed
¼ cup sugar, divided
1 large egg
½ tsp. ground cinnamon
⅓ cup finely chopped pecans or walnuts

1. Preheat oven to 400°. Unfold pastry sheets on a surface sprinkled with 2 Tbsp. sugar; roll each sheet into a 16- x 12-inch rectangle.

2. Whisk together egg and 1 Tbsp. water; brush tops of pastry sheet rectangles with half of egg mixture.

3. Combine cinnamon, pecans, and remaining 2 Tbsp. sugar; sprinkle over pastry. Starting at each shorter end, roll pastry up tightly, jelly-roll fashion, to meet in center. (The shape of the roll resembles a scroll.) Brush each with remaining egg mixture. Cut each roll into ½-inch-thick slices; place 2 inches apart on lightly greased baking sheets.

4. Bake at 400° for 10 minutes or until golden. Cool cookies on baking sheets 5 minutes. Remove to wire racks, and cool completely (about 15 minutes).

A little cinnamon and sugar and a few nuts transform puff pastry into an unbelievably tasty holiday gift.

Jam Pockets

MAKES: about 2 dozen ❋ **HANDS-ON TIME:** 15 min. ❋ **TOTAL TIME:** 1 hr., 30 min.

½ cup butter, softened
1 (3-oz.) package cream cheese, softened
1¼ cups all-purpose flour

2 Tbsp. strawberry or apricot jam
¼ cup sifted powdered sugar

1. Beat butter and cream cheese in a large mixing bowl at medium speed with an electric mixer until creamy; gradually add flour, beating until blended. Chill dough 30 minutes.

2. Preheat oven to 375°. Turn dough out onto a lightly floured surface; roll to ⅛-inch thickness, and cut with a 2-inch round cookie cutter.

3. Spoon ¼ tsp. jam into center of each dough circle; fold in half over jam, pressing edges to seal with tines of a fork. Place on a greased baking sheet.

4. Bake at 375° for 15 minutes. Cool on baking sheet 5 minutes. Remove to wire racks, and cool completely (about 25 minutes). Sprinkle with powdered sugar.

test kitchen tip: how to soften butter

■ Butter will usually soften at room temperature in about 30 minutes, but the time can vary depending on the warmth of your kitchen. Before beginning your recipe, test the butter by gently pressing the top of the stick with your index finger. If an indentation remains and the stick of butter still holds its shape (like the butter in the center), it's perfectly softened. The butter on the left is still too firm, while the butter on the right has become too soft. Avoid softening butter in the microwave, as it can melt too quickly and unevenly.

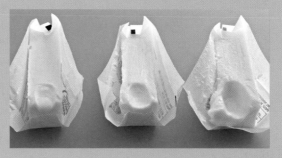

Orange Nut Balls

Coconut
Joys

Orange Nut Balls

MAKES: 5 dozen ✳ **HANDS-ON TIME:** 30 min. ✳ **TOTAL TIME:** 1 hr., 38 min.

1 cup finely chopped pecans
1 (12-oz.) package vanilla wafers
½ cup butter, melted
1 (16-oz.) package powdered sugar

1 (6-oz.) can frozen orange juice concentrate, thawed
1 (14-oz.) package sweetened flaked coconut

1. Preheat oven to 350°. Place pecans in a single layer in a shallow pan. Bake 7 to 8 minutes or until lightly toasted, stirring occasionally. Pulse vanilla wafers in a food processor 6 to 8 times or until wafers resemble fine crumbs.

2. Stir together pecans, vanilla wafer crumbs, and next 3 ingredients.

3. Shape into l-inch balls, roll in coconut, and place on a baking sheet. Cover and chill 1 hour or until firm. Store in refrigerator up to 3 weeks.

Coconut Joys

MAKES: 4 dozen ✳ **HANDS-ON TIME:** 30 min. ✳ **TOTAL TIME:** 1 hr.

3 cups sweetened flaked coconut
2 cups sifted powdered sugar
½ cup butter, melted

2 cups semisweet chocolate morsels
1 tsp. shortening

1. Stir coconut and powdered sugar into melted butter; shape into ¾-inch balls. Chill 30 minutes or until firm.

2. Microwave chocolate morsels and shortening in a medium-size microwave-safe glass bowl at HIGH 1 minute or until melted and smooth, stirring at 30-second intervals. Dip half of each coconut ball in melted chocolate mixture; place on wax paper to harden. Store in refrigerator up to 4 days.

Strawberry Fudge Balls

MAKES: 4 dozen ＊ **HANDS-ON TIME:** 15 min. ＊ **TOTAL TIME:** 1 hr., 23 min.

Put together a sampler box of flavors.

- 1 cup whole almonds
- 1 (8-oz.) package cream cheese, softened
- 1 cup semisweet chocolate morsels, melted
- ¾ cup vanilla wafer crumbs
- ¼ cup strawberry preserves

1. Preheat oven to 350°. Bake almonds in a single layer in a shallow pan 8 to 10 minutes or until lightly toasted and fragrant, stirring halfway through. Cool and finely chop.

2. Beat cream cheese at medium speed with an electric mixer until fluffy. Add melted chocolate, beating until smooth. Stir in cookie crumbs and preserves. Cover and chill 1 hour.

3. Shape mixture into 1-inch balls; roll in chopped toasted almonds. Store in an airtight container in refrigerator or freeze up to 2 months.

TRY THESE TWISTS!

Raspberry Fudge Balls: Substitute seedless raspberry preserves for strawberry preserves and pecan halves for almonds. Proceed with recipe as directed.

Apricot Fudge Balls: Substitute apricot preserves for strawberry preserves and sliced almonds, chopped, for whole almonds. Proceed with recipe as directed.

Peanut Butter Fudge Balls: Substitute chunky peanut butter for strawberry preserves and dry-roasted peanuts for almonds. Omit Step 1, and proceed with recipe as directed.

Bing Cherry Fudge Balls: Omit almonds. Substitute bing cherry preserves for strawberry preserves. Proceed with recipe as directed; roll balls in powdered sugar.

Coffee Fudge Balls: Omit almonds. Substitute coffee liqueur for strawberry preserves. Proceed with recipe as directed; roll balls in crushed dark roast coffee beans and ground chocolate.

Peanut
Butter
Fudge
Balls

Bing
Cherry
Fudge
Balls

Coffee
Fudge
Balls

Strawberry
Fudge
Balls

Cream Cheese Mints

MAKES: 8 dozen   ✳   **HANDS-ON TIME:** 1 hr., 10 min.   ✳   **TOTAL TIME:** 5 hr., 10 min.

Purchase food coloring paste at cake decorating or crafts stores.

1   (8-oz.) package cream cheese
¼   cup butter
1   (2-lb.) package powdered sugar
½   tsp. peppermint extract

¾   tsp. red food coloring paste
½   tsp. green food coloring paste
Powdered sugar

1. Cook cream cheese and butter in a saucepan over low heat, stirring constantly, until smooth. Gradually stir in 1 package powdered sugar; stir in peppermint extract.

2. Divide cream cheese mixture into 2 portions. Stir red coloring into 1 portion and green coloring into second portion.

3. Shape each portion of mixture into ¾-inch balls. Dip a snowflake-shaped cookie stamp into powdered sugar. Press each ball with stamp to flatten.

4. Let stand, uncovered, 4 hours or until firm. Freeze, if desired.

Classic Peanut Brittle

MAKES: 1 lb.   ✳   **HANDS-ON TIME:** 20 min.   ✳   **TOTAL TIME:** 25 min.

This candy is sensitive to humidity. Store it in an airtight tin to keep the candy crisp and crunchy, not sticky, to the touch.

1   cup sugar
½   cup light corn syrup
⅛   tsp. salt
1   cup dry-roasted or shelled raw peanuts

2   Tbsp. butter
1   tsp. baking soda
2   tsp. vanilla extract

1. Cook first 3 ingredients in a medium-size heavy saucepan over medium heat, stirring constantly, until mixture starts to boil. Boil, without stirring, 5 minutes or until a candy thermometer reaches 310°. Add peanuts, and cook 2 to 3 more minutes or to 280°. (Mixture should be golden brown.) Remove from heat, and stir in butter and remaining ingredients.

2. Pour into a buttered 15- x 10-inch jelly-roll pan. Spread mixture into a thin layer with the back of a wooden spoon. Let stand 5 minutes or until hardened. Break into pieces. Store in an airtight container.

TRY THESE TWISTS!

Pecan Brittle: Substitute 1 cup chopped pecans for peanuts.

Chocolate-Dipped Peanut Brittle: Prepare peanut brittle as directed. Melt 2 (2-oz.) chocolate candy coating squares; dip peanut brittle pieces into melted chocolate. Place on wax paper; let harden.

Cherry-Pistachio Bark

MAKES: 3½ lb. ✳ **HANDS-ON TIME:** 10 min. ✳ **TOTAL TIME:** 1 hr., 10 min.

2 (12-oz.) packages white chocolate morsels

6 (2-oz.) vanilla candy coating squares

1¾ cups dried cherries, divided

1½ cups chopped red or green pistachios, divided

1. Microwave chocolate morsels and candy coating in a large microwave-safe glass bowl at HIGH 3 minutes, stirring at 1-minute intervals.

2. Stir in 1¼ cups cherries and 1 cup pistachios.

3. Grease a 15- x 10-inch jelly-roll pan. Press remaining ½ cup cherries and ½ cup pistachios into chocolate mixture.

4. Chill 1 hour or until firm. Cut into pieces. Store in an airtight container up to 1 week.

Metric Equivalents

The information in the following charts is provided to help cooks outside the United States successfully use the recipes in this book. All equivalents are approximate.

EQUIVALENTS FOR DIFFERENT TYPES OF INGREDIENTS

Standard Cup	Fine Powder (ex. flour)	Grain (ex. rice)	Granular (ex. sugar)	Liquid Solids (ex. butter)	Liquid (ex. milk)
1	140 g	150 g	190 g	200 g	240 ml
¾	105 g	113 g	143 g	150 g	180 ml
⅔	93 g	100 g	125 g	133 g	160 ml
½	70 g	75 g	95 g	100 g	120 ml
⅓	47 g	50 g	63 g	67 g	80 ml
¼	35 g	38 g	48 g	50 g	60 ml
⅛	18 g	19 g	24 g	25 g	30 ml

LIQUID INGREDIENTS BY VOLUME

¼ tsp	=			1 ml
½ tsp	=			2 ml
1 tsp	=			5 ml
3 tsp	= 1 Tbsp =		½ fl oz =	15 ml
	2 Tbsp =	⅛ cup =	1 fl oz =	30 ml
	4 Tbsp =	¼ cup =	2 fl oz =	60 ml
	5⅓ Tbsp =	⅓ cup =	3 fl oz =	80 ml
	8 Tbsp =	½ cup =	4 fl oz =	120 ml
	10⅔ Tbsp =	⅔ cup =	5 fl oz =	160 ml
	12 Tbsp =	¾ cup =	6 fl oz =	180 ml
	16 Tbsp =	1 cup =	8 fl oz =	240 ml
	1 pt =	2 cups =	16 fl oz =	480 ml
	1 qt =	4 cups =	32 fl oz =	960 ml
			33 fl oz =	1000 ml = 1 l

DRY INGREDIENTS BY WEIGHT

(To convert ounces to grams, multiply the number of ounces by 30.)

1 oz	=	¹⁄₁₆ lb	=	30 g
4 oz	=	¼ lb	=	120 g
8 oz	=	½ lb	=	240 g
12 oz	=	¾ lb	=	360 g
16 oz	=	1 lb	=	480 g

LENGTH

(To convert inches to centimeters, multiply the number of inches by 2.5.)

1 in	=			2.5 cm
6 in	= ½ ft	=		15 cm
12 in	= 1 ft	=		30 cm
36 in	= 3 ft	= 1 yd	=	90 cm
40 in	=			100 cm = 1 m

COOKING/OVEN TEMPERATURES

	Fahrenheit	Celsius	Gas Mark
Freeze Water	32° F	0° C	
Room Temperature	68° F	20° C	
Boil Water	212° F	100° C	
Bake	325° F	160° C	3
	350° F	180° C	4
	375° F	190° C	5
	400° F	200° C	6
	425° F	220° C	7
	450° F	230° C	8
Broil			Grill

Index